Routledge Revivals

The Religion of the People of Israel

This book, first published in 1925, aims to demonstrate the ultimate roots of the many religious ideas of the Hebrews in Canaanite thought. This book will be of interest to students of theology and religious studies.

The Religion of the People of Israel

Rudolf Kittel

Routledge
Taylor & Francis Group

First published in 1925
by George Allen & Unwin

This edition first published in 2015 by Routledge
2 Park Square, Milton Park, Abingdon, Oxon, OX14 4RN
and by Routledge
711 Third Avenue, New York, NY 10017

Routledge is an imprint of the Taylor & Francis Group, an informa business

Publisher's Note
The publisher has gone to great lengths to ensure the quality of this reprint but points out that some imperfections in the original copies may be apparent.

Disclaimer
The publisher has made every effort to trace copyright holders and welcomes correspondence from those they have been unable to contact.

A Library of Congress record exists under LC control number: 25019293

ISBN 13: 978-1-138-91236-6 (hbk)
ISBN 13: 978-1-315-69195-4 (ebk)
ISBN 13: 978-1-138-91238-0 (pbk)

THE RELIGION OF THE PEOPLE OF ISRAEL

BY

DR. RUDOLF KITTEL

PROFESSOR AT THE UNIVERSITY OF LEIPZIG

AUTHORIZED TRANSLATION BY

R. CARYL MICKLEM

LONDON: GEORGE ALLEN & UNWIN LTD.
RUSKIN HOUSE, 40 MUSEUM STREET, W.C. 1

First published in 1925

Printed in Great Britain

TRANSLATOR'S FOREWORD

I HOPE this translation will prove to be of value to many students, and to other readers who may be interested in the subject.

My best thanks are due to Dr. Kittel for his courtesy in allowing me to translate his book, and for the kindly interest which he has shown in my undertaking. My warm thanks are also due to Professor Charlotte Knoch for her careful and valuable revision of my translation. And to my brother, the Rev. N. Micklem, M.A., Professor of Old Testament Literature and Theology at the Selly Oak Colleges, I am deeply indebted for all the encouragement and help he has so freely given—without which I should never have ventured on the task of translation.

R. CARYL MICKLEM.

NORTHRIDGE, BOXMOOR, HERTS.
September, 1924.

PREFACE

THIS book is the outcome of lectures which I delivered at the invitation of the Olaus-Petri Foundation at the University of Upsala in the spring of 1920. I was not so much concerned to expound the details of my subject as to weld closely the threads of the general development, and to demonstrate its inherent forces. In distinction from the usual presentation of the subject I have also kept my aim in view to demonstrate the ultimate roots of many religious ideas of the Hebrews in Canaanite thought. My exposition intentionally goes back beyond the strictly Israelite early history and describes first, in a chapter of its own, the Canaanite religion as that which was indigenous in the land. The result of this is surprisingly illuminating, as the language (including the religious) and the culture of the Canaanites were simply adopted by the Israelites; so many of the Canaanite religious ideas exercised a much stronger religious influence over Israel than one usually supposes.

In many respects Israel's religion thereby takes on a new colour.

It will not escape the notice of anyone who follows carefully the author's exposition that it lingers with particular sympathy over that point where a people, utterly broken and robbed of all power, found means to recover and to start life afresh solely because of their faith in themselves and in their future. May this little book find readers who are prepared to be instructed by the lessons of history!

I did not feel called upon to discuss Friedr. Delitzsch's unattractive new book *Die grosse Täuschung*. Those who desire to know my opinion concerning it I refer to the fourth edition (1920) of my *Alttest. Wissenschaft*, which is being published simultaneously with this volume. Here I call attention primarily to my remarks on pages 91, 100, 141, 161–2.

R. KITTEL.

LEIPZIG,
October 1920.

CONTENTS

THE RELIGION OF THE PEOPLE OF ISRAEL

CHAPTER I

THE CANAANITE BACKGROUND—THE INDIGENOUS RELIGION

THE SIGNIFICANCE OF CANAAN.

From whence the Israelites came is to a large degree veiled in mystery. It is hardly probable that they came from a single province or community. They are much more likely to have gathered from several different provinces, from the east as well as from the south. So also the influences, which go to the building up of the Hebrew religion in the form in which it is presented to us in the history of the Israelites, did not flow from one single source, but were derived from various sources.

Many questions remain unanswered with regard to their ultimate origin. On the other hand, it is quite certain that the Hebrew religion in historical times took shape on the soil of Palestine or *Canaan*, and in close connexion with the religion of the country.

It was here that the people's lot was cast since the time of Moses, it was here also that its religious life unfolded, it was here that according to tradition, whether in the land itself or on its borders, the tribes of its patriarchs had already dwelt. If tradition can be corroborated, then the religious life and thought of those ancestral tribes must have developed even in those days in frequent touch, and perhaps in contrast, with that of the Canaanites.

Thus we are shown the door through which alone we are able to investigate the religion of Israel. It is certain without qualification that the great factor from which we must seek to understand the post-Mosaic, and perhaps even the very earliest religion of Israel, is the religion of Canaan. Perhaps the religion of Moses and of his time may have been influenced from elsewhere, namely, from Arabia, the word being taken in its broadest sense. But Canaan was also near enough to the wilderness, and everything that after Moses' time contributed to the Hebrew religion or influenced it from foreign sources, whether from Babylon or from Asia Minor or from anywhere else, for centuries came to it through the mediation of the Canaanites.

Before the time of Solomon it was most exceptional for the Israelites to have immediate contact with the great civilizations. Thus it is proper that we first examine the Canaanite religion. At every turn we shall come into contact with the Hebrew religion of the Old Testament which will facilitate the understanding of our proper subject.[1]

Pre-Semitic Religion.

The oldest forms of worshipping non-earthly or, at least, non-human beings on Canaanite soil appear to go back to the primeval pre-Semitic times. To

[1] On this whole section cf. Kittel, *Geschichte d. Volk. Israel*, I[3] (1916), pp. 112–238 (= I[5, 6], [1923], pp. 89–91).

estimate years or centuries is useless; enough to know that we certainly find them far into the third if not the fourth millennium before Christ. What we find here may be designated as simple polydemonism. Certain funeral customs in Gezer, by which an attempt was made utterly to destroy the body by burning, point to a primitive belief in a soul, namely, the conception of a soul within the body being inextricably bound up with it and able to cause trouble so long as the body continues to exist. In this period of the more ancient great stone monuments the cultus was practised, as far as we can see, chiefly at cromlechs or circles of stone (Gilgal?) and at menhirs or stone pillars and roughly pointed or upright stone blocks such as Jacob's stone at Bethel was thought to be. What form of religious worship was practised within the precincts of a holy place or at the upright stone blocks cannot accurately be told. Nevertheless it may be taken for granted that gifts were brought to the earth spirits and to the ancestral spirits who dwelt in these sacred spots. We have little information as to the nature of these gifts. From certain basin or dish-shaped cavities in stones and flat rocks drink-offerings seem most probable. Although many of these peculiar dishes may have served everyday purposes, a number of them can be explained only as showing the sacrificial dishes in which water, oil, and probably also wine and blood were brought to the spirits of earth, of springs, and perhaps even of fertility that dwelt in the neighbourhood.

Thus in all probability we are introduced to the oldest form of sacrifice in Palestine. Men simply placed their gift before the demon or god and left it to him to fetch it away. This procedure finds its way into the Old Testament; thus we already have here an example of the significance which the most primitive world of Canaan possesses for the understanding of Biblical religion.[1]

The Semites.

All this still belongs to pre-Semitic times. With the incursion of the Semites not only did customs with regard to the dead change, but many customs connected with sacrifice and many religious views. The dead were now buried. All kinds of offerings, especially food and drink, show that they would continue their existence down below as they had lived here. So it came about that they were treated, perhaps not exactly with true worship, yet certainly reverentially, as becomes mysterious beings of an invisible world. Peculiar sacrificial customs such as human, especially child-sacrifice, and sacrifice when a house was built are not undisputed, but eminently probable.[2] So far as it is attested, the immuring of human beings in buildings would seem to give most probable evidence of the continued life of those earth-spirits in the belief of the Semites also: the life sacrificed was intended to satisfy the spirit as the possessor of the place and at the same time to protect future inhabitants from him; here we have the earliest, still absolutely naturalistic basis of the thought of redemption and propitiation. There was still a vast distance to travel before propitiation was grounded in ethics.

The Root Ideas of Clean and Unclean.

It may, perhaps, seem strange to many if we here call attention to certain ideas and customs that were

[1] Judges vi. 11 ff.

[2] A scholar who has recently died, F. Schwally, has stigmatized this idea as "nonsensical". He has overlooked the fact that it is remarkably confirmed by the conduct of Hiel in the rebuilding of Jericho as recorded in 1 Kings xvi. 34.

powerful in later Israel. But they are only intelligible in the light of the stimulus of the belief in spirits in this earliest period and in the efforts of the Yahweh religion to prevent its continuance. The tenacity with which these primitive ideas continue to live is well known in all religions. If, for Yahweh's sake, a number of things were declared to be unclean in later Israel, the key to the prohibition is often found exclusively in the circumstance that such things or customs were forbidden, *tabu*, because they were intimately associated with that primitive religion which in principle had been overcome, but which still played a part in the life of many individuals.

Thus, much later times, as well as the data provided by the excavations, are an important source for the knowledge of primitive times. If we learn that the feeding of the dead was forbidden in Israel, our former observation concerning it is confirmed. If we see that contact with dead bodies or entering into a house in which a death had taken place or many other customs connected with the dead were defiling, as similarly birth, leprosy, and all sorts of secretions and processes of the human body, they are *tabu*, simply because in the days when the belief in spirits and kindred sinister powers was universal, these things were subject to their particular influence. The same belief accounts for certain intrinsically edible animals being looked upon as unclean, for certain people being kept away from military camps, for a portion of the harvest being reserved for the field spirits, and for many similar things. In saying this I do not wish to infer that all these customs and ideas were already fully developed in these earliest days, but they all have their origin here, and therefore are intelligible only in the light of these primitive times.

THE DEITY.

In connexion with sacrifice the custom of simply placing the offering for the gods to carry away seems at first to have been continued, but the Semitic dwellers in Canaan seem more and more to have superseded it, and to have gone over to the practice of burning the sacrificial gifts. Perhaps the stately stone altar, which still stands at Samson's birthplace, Zorea, and also the altar-like stone block excavated by Sellin in Taanak even then served such a purpose. At all events the change is closely connected with a fundamental change in view-point: a god takes the place of a spirit-being.

This leads us inevitably to the question of the Godhead itself. Gods properly so called are in no way presupposed by the above-mentioned traces of religious or quasi-religious life. Only impersonal or half-personal local spirit-beings after the manner of the spirits of the dead are implied. How far many primitive idols, which existed here and there in Palestine, prove more it is difficult to say, and in no case with certainty. The word "god" we hear for the first time at the end of the third and the beginning of the second millennium, and that, too, from a foreign source. A Babylonian colonist in Canaan, or more likely a true Canaanite, Atanaḫili, pronounces himself a worshipper of Nergal, that is, a worshipper of a Babylonian god of mischance. Nergal, however, was no mere demon; he was a god proper. We may assume that neither Atanaḫili nor his god Nergal stood alone. Simultaneously, or soon after him (Atanaḫili) others, including natives, will have followed his example.

Beside Nergal, Ishtar-Ashtart and other foreign deities will soon have celebrated their entry into the land,[1] especially among the steadily increasing Semitic population. So much the more remarkable seems the fact that up to the present time we know of no kind of pictorial representation of the deity at that period. This would lead us to suppose that the oldest Semites in Canaan like the oldest Arabs had, on principle or in fact, repudiated divine images.

We know of the Hyksos that they brought with them, at the time of their invasion into Egypt, their own god which the Egyptians called Sutech. Now this Sutech corresponds to the Canaanite Baal. From this we may safely assume that the Baal, with which the Old Testament and other sources have made us so familiar, was worshipped in Canaan between 2000 and 1500 B.C., indeed even earlier by an isolated few.[2]

Besides Baal his female counterpart Baalah or Ashtart would not have been lacking. And since we can infer from old place-names the worship not only of this Baalah but also of 'Anat, as also of the sun and the moon, there is nothing to prevent our attributing their introduction to this period. Hadad and Ramman may have entered the land at the same time as the Assyrian 'Anat, but for the most part to be incorporated in Baal.

SPIRIT AND GOD.

This course of events agrees with what was said above. Probably Baal and his like were previously nothing more than local spirit-beings. Their later character unmistakably shows their origin. We do not know what the pre-Semitic people called these earth and water spirits. The Semites who invaded

[1] So also Nabu and probably Sin too (cf. the names Nebo and Sin given to mountains) and others.

[2] Cf. *Gesch.*, I^3, pp. 211, 216, c. 216^7 (I$^{5, 6}$, pp. 170, 174, c. 174^8), together with the next note.

the land called them in their own language Baal and Baalah, i.e. possessor, male and female.[1]

But since real "gods" were known in the land, Baal and Baalah were no longer able to hold their old position. Certainly they remained for many what they had been, but simultaneously a change was effected. What holds good in the case of Nergal, Shemesh, 'Anat, and Hadad, seems to apply equally to Baal and Baalah. Baal was associated with Shemesh and became the sun god, Baalah the moon goddess. Gods of sun, moon and firmament were developed from a power which makes earth, trees, and flocks fruitful and from demons of fertility and vegetation.

The change was effected so much the more easily as the sun and light of themselves represent the elements that promote life and vegetation. It may well be only an accident that we learn of Baal as the god of thunder and of vegetation from Egyptian sources in the second half of the second millennium.[2] Certainly he had undergone this change in the motherland, Canaan ; the earth and water spirit had thereby become god of fertility, of the sun, and of the heavens.

For a long time through the mediation of the mercantile coast towns various influences of higher civilization, from Egypt on the one hand and Babylon on the other, had made themselves felt in the land. But since the final conquest of the country by Thutmes III, when it was converted into an Egyptian province, Egyptian civilization and culture permeated the entire country.

The Amarna period produced a copious literature

[1] We have evidence of the Baalah of Byblos from 2500 B.C., vide *Gesch.*, I[3], p. 218[7] (I[5, 6], p. 176[6]).

[2] Cf. Gressmann in Baudissin's *Festschrift*, 1918, pp. 191 ff.

which was written in the Babylonian language and script. Archives were common in the land here and there, even in small towns.[1] Names such as " City of Books " or " City of Writers " lead us to suppose that the guild of the literate was widespread, not only for traditional foreign diplomatic writing, but also for home alphabetic writing which, since the time of Hyksos, had developed from the Egyptian writing. Babylonian myths no less than indigenous Canaanite hymns and psalms were heard here and there at the courts of princes or in the circle of the priestly guilds at the sanctuaries.

All this shows us that increasingly, especially since the middle of the second millennium, namely, since the time when we may presume to see the first traces of the children of Israel in their infancy, an upper class of the population in Palestine appears which was far removed from primitive forms of life and manners of thought. This could not but be fruitful for religion.

THE CONCEPTION OF GOD.

It is significant that the word " god " can be traced for the first time in Canaan in connexion with a foreign deity.

Atanaḫili (" I sigh, my god ") was, as we learn, a worshipper of the Babylonian Nergal. We do not know how old the word *el* is in Canaan.[2] It was among the primitive words of the Semites, for it was handed down from the time when they still lived together ; it probably signified nothing more than the Mighty One, the Powerful One, so that it may well have been used of those spirit-beings which the Semites

[1] *Gesch.*, I[3], pp. 196 ff. (I[5,6], p. 165[5]), and under heading " Archiv " in the index.

[2] We can trace El much earlier in Babylon. *Gesch.*, I[3], p. 206[1] (I[5,6], pp. 156 ff.).

adopted from their predecessors in the land of Canaan. But at present the only fact which is certain is that the word *el* appears in Canaan for the first time about 2000 B.C., and that Atanaḫili uses it to designate the Babylonian Nergal.

What Idea does the Word "El" convey here?

In all religions the conception of God is determinative of the character of the religion itself. So the answer to our question must be of fundamental significance for the religion of ancient Canaan.

It is highly probable, as we have already seen, that the Canaanites, like the Semites in general, looked upon God as the Mighty One. Experience had early taught that man on earth and beyond is face to face with superior powers to whom he is subject, and whose favour he must endeavour to gain. People only expressed experiences which each day seemed to verify, when they traced back such experiences to invisible powers, *elîm*.

But the chief question for us now is that of the more exact meaning of this title. Is *el*, God, a proper name, or is it a generic term? As a matter of fact we occasionally meet in Syria—not, however, until after the year 1000 B.C.—an individual god *el*, who bears the name El as a proper name.[1] Further, we meet in ancient Canaan, as in the Bible, a large number of pre-Israelite names compounded with *el* which prove that a deity was frequently worshipped among the ancient Canaanite tribes under the title of *el*. In the Old Testament we find such names as Isma-el, Jeraḥme-el, Re'u-el, Betu-el, probably also names like Metusha-el, Mechuja-el; such names as Milki-ili or Il-milki,

[1] In the Hadad inscription of Sendshirli and in the Panammu inscription, cf. Lidzbarski, *Nordsemitische Epigraphik*, pp. 214 f.

Jabne-il, Rab-ili, have been handed down to us especially through the Amarna tablets, and even earlier, from other sources about 1500 B.C., Ja'qob-el, Josef-el. Attempts have been made to construe these names as well as certain Babylonian proper names of similar construction, some of a much earlier date, on the supposition that *el* was the proper name of an individual god. But it is not so. At any rate there is no certain proof that *el* was here used as indicating anything more than an appellative, as anything more than a kind of generic term. Of course, this god probably had a name, but it was not *el*, but some other name such as Nergal, Sin and so on.

We must insist, therefore, that before the first millennium the word *el* was used on non-Biblical Canaanite soil to signify God and the Godhead generally, but not to designate a definite, individual god, while in Israel Elohim or El was very commonly used as a proper name for Yahweh.

If this last idea be followed out consistently, it is found essentially to imply that this God Yahweh is in fact God absolutely, that is, the only God. It was precisely this consciousness which was lacking in ancient Canaan. We find the plural *elim*; indeed, quite a pantheon is known and worshipped. Every one of these deities could, of course, equally claim his right to the generic title *el*.

Baal.

The most important among the Canaanite gods was, as we have seen, Baal. Fundamentally the name possessor, owner, implies that it is not a question of a particular god of this name, but is a generic term, and, as a matter of fact, there was not one, but there were many baals.

Each place had its own baal. The name is an old one in Babylon. Since the time of Sargon I and Naramsin we find there proper names which most probably point to the worship of a western-Semitic god Baal.[1] He must have been brought to Canaan by the Amorites, and there took the place of the native belief in spirits and transformed it. Local earth spirits, water spirits, and spirits of fertility, in which the primitive pre-Semitic dwellers in the land believed, he transformed into gods of fertility, or rather gods who as possessors of the land and at the same time as gods of thunder, sun, sky and life, were looked upon as distributors of the gifts and products of the earth and of the progeny of man and beast.[2]

Since the time when Baal, from being an impersonal spirit, became a personal god, it is a matter of course that he, like other gods, had his female counterpart. Accordingly she was called, as we already know, Baalah, female of possessor.[3]

Naturally she had exactly the same offices to perform as her consort Baal. But at this point an unexpected, and at the same time noteworthy, change took place. When Bel-Marduk came over from the East and became Baal, it was only a matter of course that his female counterpart Ishtar should come too. And when Baal acquired his consort like the gods proper, she also became the Baalah, a goddess. That is to say, not only from an impersonal being, one might almost say from a principle, a personal being was developed, but at the same time a generic title became a proper name. From Baal in general, regarded as an undefined being, grew "the Baal" absolutely, as a definite individual who represented the genus. And

[1] *Gesch.*, I[3], p. 211[1] (5, 6, p. 170[4]). [2] Ibid., p. 218 (5, 6, p. 175[6]).
[3] Ibid., p. 218[7] (5, 6, p. 176[6]).

correspondingly it was not long before the Baalah acquired an independent proper name, Ashtart. The name became so familiar that, except in Byblos and at Sinai, the Baalah falls almost entirely into the background, and in her place the Baal, who remained firmly rooted from of yore, frequently had Ashtart at his side.

ASHTART.

Her primary, although not exclusive, province was physical fertility in man and beast. Like the Babylonian Ishtar, and like the Asia Minor and Thracian Great Mother of the gods, she was the goddess of sensuous love and the patroness of generative and growing life. The great mystery of life seemed to these peoples so profoundly a matter of religious awe that they were unable to interpret its origin and its hidden motions and activities in man and beast, and indeed the whole of sexual life, except as being under the protection and guidance of a single great deity. Unfortunately the great, eternal truth, which here seeks expression, namely, that procreation is an act sacred and proper to the presence of God, in practice was frequently degraded. Acts in imitation of the deity were regarded as service to the god. Like Ishtar, Ashtart had a number of men and women ministrants who were described as consecrated persons, qedeshah, qadesh.[1] They consecrated themselves in her service to prostitution. The idea, elevated and pure in itself, was thereby surrendered to the lower instincts. Those who know the power of these instincts over mankind can form some idea of the devastating sway which this religious practice exerted over the people of the Further East. In the Old Testament Ashtart often bears the name Ashêrah in this connexion.

[1] *Gesch.*, I³, p. 222 (I⁵·⁶, p. 178).

THE PANTHEON.

It is beyond the scope of this sketch to describe here each individual god of the Canaanite pantheon. Enough that we mention the most important names and add a few remarks about them.

A few names have already been mentioned because they may have been longer known in the land, for instance, 'Anath, which is familiar to us from place-names such as Anathoth and Bethany (Beth'anath). She is represented with spear and shield, and is therefore a war goddess. Already under Thutmes III she had a priesthood in Thebes. In addition to 'Anath there were Hadad ('Adad) and Ramman. They were closely related and were in reality the same deity; it is the weather and vegetation god. 'Adad, as the god of thunder, made the heavens to tremble.[1] As his symbol he carried the axe, which split the heavens asunder, and the lightning sheaf; his animal was the bull, the prototype of generative power. As Ramman or Rimmon, as he was called in Israel, he frequently appears in Hebrew place-names. A figure of a bull at Er-Rummane in the country on the east of the Jordan bears witness to him to this day. If 'Adad-Ramman played an important part in the Babylonian pantheon, this is no less true of the sun-god Shamash, known in Canaan as Shemesh, and of the moon-god Sin. The former we find in place-names such as Beth-shemesh; for an example of the latter we may, in all probability, point to Mount Sinai and to the wilderness of Sin. The moon-god, Jareach, is probably contained in the name of the city of Jericho.

[1] According to Gressmann (op. cit., p. 207), Baal should be substituted for him in the Amarna texts. In fact he is incorporated in Baal.

Further deities brought from Babylon are Nabu or Nebo, the spokesman of the gods, the previously mentioned Nergal, and also deities of good fortune like Gad. It would seem, indeed, that there are bound up in the particular deities even at this time certain ethical ideas, such as Ṣedeq, righteousness and justice, and Shalem, peace. The name Shipti-Baal may also be mentioned in this connexion.

EGYPTIAN INFLUENCE. ADONIS.

Strong as Babylonian influence was upon the Canaanite religion as far back as shortly after the year 2000 B.C., the Egyptian influence, especially since the time of Thutmes III (about 1500 B.C.), was no less important. The government officials and troops who lived in the country since Thutmes' time will have brought their Egyptian gods with them, and the traders and merchants who followed them in greater numbers will have done likewise. The Egyptian vassals at the royal courts as well as those among the masses throughout the country considered it a matter of course that in religion also they should be subservient to the ruling powers.[1] Just as the native goddess Ashtart had been long worshipped in the form of the Egyptian Hathor,[2] so we meet with traces of the worship of the Egyptian god Amon, especially after the Amarna period. Canaanites were frequently named after him, and on the other hand the Egyptians could remind a Syrian that his fathers had long ago recognized Amon as their lord. Indeed, some of the Pharaoh's Syrian vassals went so far as to break out

[1] *Gesch.*, I[3], pp. 232 f. (5, 6, 186 f.), except that the information in p. 233 (5, 6, 187[5]) to be corrected according to Weber in *Knudtzon El-Amarnatafeln*, p. 1158.

[2] Cf., for example, illustration 10 in Kittel, *Die altiest. Wissensch.*[4] (1920), p. 57.

into formal hymns and exultations of praise to the Egyptian sun-god king.[1]

We must expect that the gods of the Hittites were not lacking, on account of the influence which the Hittites had in the land, especially after the Amarna period. In the north we find the Aramaic god Ramman-Hadad in the form of the Hittite Teshub, and in the south the Prince of Jerusalem called himself Ḥipa, after the Hittite goddess. We find the same name Abdiḥiba also in Taanak, that is, in central Palestine.

In closest relationship to Baal is a deity that the Canaanites called Adon, "lord", or Adoni, "my lord", and which we know through the Greeks as Adonis. He was, like the Egyptian Osiris and the Babylonian Tammuz, a god of vegetation; the death and re-birth of Nature in winter and spring was thought to have been represented by the fate of the youth torn by wild beasts, but later brought to life again. Little flower gardens planted in his honour represented his fate.

We know the cult of Adonis fairly well from later Phœnician times through Philo of Byblos and Alexander Polyhistor. But as the Old Testament contains many allusions to him,[2] we must take for granted that Adonis was in vogue at the time when the Israelites were in Canaan, and that he forced his way into Israel at the same time as and as a part of the baal-worship. Hence it is almost certain that the cult was practised in ancient Canaanite times, for which there is some independent evidence. People probably thought, as in Egypt of Osiris, so in Canaan of Adonis, that not

[1] *Gesch.*, I3, pp. 212[1], 232 f. (I5, 6, pp. 171[2], 186 f).

[2] Hos. vi. 2; 1 Kings xii. 24; lxx. probably; also Isa. xvii. 10.; vide *Gesch.*, I3, p. 236[3] (I5, 6, p. 190[1]).

only he himself came to life again, but with him his worshippers also. The dead were treated at their funeral celebrations as if they themselves were Adonis.[1] It cannot be gainsaid that these facts, properly estimated, may possibly be invoked to give a partially new basis for the much discussed problem of the fate of the dead in Israelite thought.

CONCLUSION.

If without examining more closely the many lesser deities, we draw the conclusion to which we may now come, we unmistakably have a well-developed mixed religion which we are accustomed to call by the ineradicable but misleading word " syncretism." The religion entirely conforms to the geographical position of the country and to its subsequent historical development. From the middle or end of the third millennium native elements mixed with those of the Babylonians, of the Egyptians, of the Hittites and of other peoples. Moreover, it follows that when they gave up the belief in spirits or, more accurately, when the gods took their places beside the spirits or in many cases displaced them, we have before us an out-and-out polytheism. It is a matter of course that the primitive polydæmonism continued to exist among the masses in the country, not only at this time but until much later times. But the upper classes are everywhere those who determine the further development of a religion.

Yet the polytheism in Canaan was not of precisely the same kind as elsewhere. In order to appraise it correctly we must go back constantly to its fundamental type, the worship of Baal. Many as were the gods introduced from without, they were not able to change the fundamental character of the religion as a

[1] Baudissin, *Adonis and Eschmun*, 1911, pp. 90–91.

baal-worship. The Old Testament furnishes us with the clearest proof of this when it represents Baal and Ashtart, or merely the baals, as comprehending Canaanite heathendom.

To be sure, the baal religion, too, was a nature religion, and that in a marked degree, but it differed from the ordinary nature religion in that Baal was not a natural force or an expression of nature personally conceived, such as the lightning, the sun, the moon, when they were regarded as deities ; Baal in conformity with his origin from the earth-spirits and water-spirits is and remains the possessor and owner of the earth, the spring or the tree. So in course of time he may well have become associated with the sun, and his female counterpart with the moon ; people may consequently have spoken occasionally of Shemesh or of Sin and similar beings as independent gods and indeed as proper personifications of those natural bodies ; in this case, the sun, the moon and lightning were really conceived personally.

But this was the foreign, not the original and indigenous way of thinking, according to which Shemesh, Sin and Baraq are only baals. Baal, however, through all his changes was never represented except as lord and possessor. The dominant conception, which was bound up with that deity, was and remained not the personification of nature, but the possession and ownership of a place or of an object. Just as every field, every tree had its possessor and every town its prince, so close to or behind the agricultural or princely possessor stood invisible the divine owner and ruler of land, tree, river and town. So the sun, the moon and the heavens had their own baal also. Again, these baals were not the personification of the heavenly bodies personally conceived, but rather the invisible powers behind them. The baal Tamar was not the palm-tree personified, but the baal *at* it.[1] The spring baalah was the baalah *at* the spring. The baal of the heavens was he who rules in the heavens and who at the same time dwells there.[2] The sun baal was the lord and master of the sun who directed it in its course.[3]

As I have already emphasized, this does not imply that there were not other ideas regarding these things in Canaan. It is much more a question of the proper and normal ideas connected with the thought of Baal. If this coincides with the line of thought presented here, then the results are not without significance.

The Inter-Relations of the Gods.

We cannot, however, leave the question of the Canaanite idea of God without alluding to the problem of the mutual relations of the gods, whether they are called *el* or baal.

The question may be most clearly decided with regard to *el*. We have rejected the opinion that everywhere in ancient Canaanite times *el* represented a definite, single god in any other sense than that each particular worshipper might call the tutelary deity, under whose protection he stood, God simply. So it may have been that Atanaḥili had Nergal, or Ilmilki another god or baal among the many, for his private favourite god.[4]

But this does not solve the problem. The mere fact is significant that in Canaan as in Babylon it had

[1] Judges xx. 33.

[2] Hence he was also called Baal in the heavens. *Gesch.*, I^3, p. 218^5 ($I^{5, 6}$, p. 176^4).

[3] It is natural to compare Ps. xix. 5 f., the thought is here intentionally modified; the sun functions at the behest of Yahweh.

[4] Compare the change in *Gesch.*, I^3, p. 209^{1-2} ($I^{5, 6}$, p. 168^{2-3}).

become common custom to use a generic name in place of a proper name for a god. The reader may put to himself the question, what goes on within the human soul which says, "I sigh (to thee), my god", instead of "I sigh (to thee), Nergal", and instead of "such and such a god grants increase, grants reward", to say "God grants increase, God grants reward"?

Such a substitution of a generic word for a single being is, I believe, only conceivable when in a particular circle one definite god seems to tower above the others to such a degree that for his worshippers he becomes simply "the god", "the baal", and consequently God absolutely. For others, and for the people as a whole, that god may play an unimportant part. So for one person Nergal may have played this part, for others Marduk or Ashtart.

But the thought is ever the same: this god is to me *the* god, the one who means more than all the others to me. This alone explains how *el* could finally become a proper name, although, as far as we know at present, it was not recognized as such outside the Bible until after the year 1000 B.C.

In addition, however, we now have to face the fact that the Egyptian vassal kings in Canaan went so far in their subjection to the royal dreamer in Thebes that they gave up their native polytheism for the monotheistic thought of the sun-king, as well as the second fact that it was customary in Taanak at the same time to speak of the "lord of the gods", just as in Babylon it had long been the custom to speak of the "king of the gods". We can have no doubt, therefore, that in Canaan, as in the East, the worship of many gods was known under the form of monarchic polytheism. A head or chief god was raised up above the others. This was the first effective step towards monotheism. Doubtless one must not set too much store by this first evidence. It may have been a mere phrase or gesture of politeness. But the evidence from Taanak proves that the gesture found followers and provoked many to meditation.

SPIRITUALIZATION.

Strange as it may sound, it would also seem as if a few deeply penetrating minds in Canaan at this time were advancing to a kind of speculative spiritualization of polytheism which brought them close to the borders of belief in one God. At least, a further fact can scarcely be explained in any other way, the remarkable fact that the Hebrew word *elohim*, their principal name for God, is a plural form, but has been rendered innocuous in the Old Testament, as is well known, in that, contrary to all rules of grammar, this plural is construed with the singular of the predicate or of the attribute. By this means the Hebrews sought to explain that this plural is merely a matter of form: God is singular. Exactly the same is known in ancient Canaan as an exceptional case, but not as a rule.[1] It was certainly true only of a thoughtful minority. This we must energetically emphasize for this whole range of ideas.

But how was it with Jesus and his followers and with Luther amongst their contemporaries when they made their appearance? And what did this minority accomplish? For Canaan it must suffice that for such a group not only did one god tower above all others, but that the Godhead was occasionally even looked upon as a unity.

[1] Böhl, *Die Sprache der Amarna-briefe*, 1905, pp. 35 f.; Kittel, *Gesch.*, I[3], p. 214 (I[5, 6], pp. 173 f.).

El-Elyon.

From this viewpoint we shall scarcely be able to regard it as insignificant that it was precisely Jerusalem, whose prince Abdiḫiba acknowledged the solar monotheism of Pharaoh at the Amarna period, that appears elsewhere also as a place where there was an idea pointing towards the unity of God. Its priest-king Melkiṣedeq, according to Genesis xiv., would seem to have been a believer in El-Elyon, the most High God, the Creator of heaven and earth. This figure of Melkiṣedeq is much disputed and cannot be accepted with full assurance, but the evidence which we have apart from the Bible certainly heightens the probability of his historical character. Besides the analogies already mentioned the witness of Philo of Byblos especially demands consideration. He speaks of a god Eliun called the Highest, Hypsistos, of whom he moreover tells us that he with *Berut* created heaven and earth. Berut means nothing more than Berytos (Beirut), so that Eliun seems to stand in close relationship to the Adonis worshipped in Byblos. His name Elyon may originally have meant simply the " Lofty One ", that is, the baal of heaven, but as he came to be designated Creator God, he appears to have risen more and more to the rank of the Most High, Hypsistos. Corroborating this is his association with the all-powerful Shaddai by Balaam, where curiously enough we find the proper name *el* in connexion with the same god at this very time.[1] The Balaam oracles are not of earlier date than Saul, and are consciously intended to give the primitive Aramaic-Canaanite idea of God. Their testimony therefore is not without weight.

[1] Num. xxiv. 16.

CULTUS.

We come finally to the cultus and religious thought of ancient Canaan.

The familiar name for the place of sacrifice is sufficiently well known to us from the Old Testament. It is called high place, *bamah*. This points to a time when people liked to think of the Godhead as appearing or revealing himself on prominent heights, and also explains how many holy places came to have such names as Ramah, Gibeah, Mispah—Height, Hill, Watch-tower. I do not wish to infer that the name bamah has always borne that significance. It would almost seem as though it had first found favour when people connected Baal with the heavens, for on the heights and mountains man is brought nearest to the sun and to the heavens. We know likewise the apparatus of the high place; Baal and Ashtart's most important insignia are the *massebah* and *asherah*. The first was originally a roughly prepared stone pillar, which in course of time probably became less and less crude. In ancient times this was considered the actual abode of the spirit-being, and as such was called Beth-el, god's dwelling-place; when *elim* or baals rose to the rank of gods, it became more and more the symbol and guarantee of the god's presence. So it could be a substitute for the image.

Baal was present in his symbol. The same applies to Ashtart in respect of the *asherah*. As goddess of fertility she was represented with the fruit-tree as her emblem, a post or tree-trunk stuck into the earth. Where a proper tree was available, the *asherah* will have been dispensed with in earlier times.[1] If the

[1] Cf. the familiar formula in connexion with the cult at the high places "(on every high hill and) under every green tree." Deut. xii. 2, 1 Kings xiv. 23.

tree was wanting, an artificial equivalent had to be fashioned. It cannot be an accident that this emblem of Ashtart bears the name which is occasionally ascribed to the goddess herself, even though the connexion has not yet been fully explained.

ALTAR.

In the earliest period there was no need for an altar. As long as those *elim* or baals were worshipped as spirit-beings, it was enough to place the gifts for them on the places where they were pleased to dwell. For this purpose a flat rock was sufficient, or a rough stone block, or the holy tree, upon the branches of which people hung, as is customary to this day, what they intended for the god. We still read of a similar proceeding in the case of Gideon in the Book of Judges.[1] For the slaughter a rough, unhewn, stone block was quite enough; upon this the blood was poured, or an altar was made of earth such as was prescribed by the ancient Hebrew law concerning altars.[2] But a change was effected when Baal became god, and, indeed, god of heaven, and the places for worship were transferred from spring, field and tree to the high places. A god who dwelt in the heavens, and who only appeared here from time to time when he was called upon, would scorn to have to fetch away his gifts from the sacred place. He would have them sent after him. And he was no longer so crudely conceived as to be supposed to consume them as they were. People burnt them and let them ascend to him in sacrificial smoke. This was the first step towards the spiritualization, or at least towards the disembodiment, of the Godhead. Moreover it became

[1] Judges vi. 11 ff.

[2] Exod. xx. 24; 1 Sam. xiv. 33.

evident that for such sacrifices a proper hearth was necessary. In place of the gift-table and slaughter-stone a proper altar-hearth was erected.

The Significance of Sacrifice.

The question as to the earliest meaning underlying sacrifice is still much debated. One readily supposes that it originally represents a magical compulsion which man sought to exercise upon the Godhead. In our field this supposition finds only limited confirmation. As far as we are able to gather from our sources about the meaning of the celebrations, the Canaanite sacrifices, like those of the Israelites, must have been essentially feasts of communion with God. The great value laid upon the meal, the common feasting upon the sacrificial victim, whereby the god was thought to be present and the worshippers to be his guests,[1] together with the profuse indulgence in wine, which lent a strongly orgiastic character to the feast and might lead the celebrations to degenerate into wild, delirious intoxication—all this proves that the object of the sacrificial feast was less the compulsion of the godhead than the god's entering into the worshippers up to the point of ecstasy, that is, up to the point of closest communion. This at least was the case with a proper meal-sacrifice. It may have been quite otherwise in the case of a proper burnt-offering, which however was of later date. We find an example of such a sacrifice in the Baal worshippers on Carmel. Here the self-mutilation and the whole character of the sacrifice to implore the god do indeed point to ideas closely related to magical compulsion; yet the interpretation is not perfectly clear; it is also very questionable how old this particular kind

[1] *Gesch.*, I[3], p. 247 (I[5, 6], pp. 199 f.).

of sacrifice was in Canaan. Unfortunately we do not know in the least.

FESTIVALS.

With regard to the festivals,[1] we have every reason primarily to consider the three more ancient of the annual Biblical feasts, for they are bound up with the soil. In spring when the sickle was first put into the crops, in early summer when the wheat was ripe, and in autumn when the fruits of the vineyards and orchards were gathered in, people assembled at the local sanctuaries for the feast to bring the native deities, the baals, thank-offerings for the blessings of the year and to make merry. This will have been the common rule. Together with these all kinds of separate feasts may have been going on, which later were either not at all or only partially adopted by Israel. In Shechem an ancient dedication feast seems to have been common, a kind of marriage festival of the fields. In Shiloh the maidens were wont to keep a feast with maiden dances in the vineyards, probably in honour of the baalah. In Gilead another such rite, a dirge ceremony, was held, very likely for a dead goddess; later this was transferred to Jephthah's daughter. We have already pointed out that in all probability the mourning for Adonis or Tammuz was known even in ancient times.

Also all manner of consecration rites would seem to have been practised. A particular god of contracts, the *baal berith,* leads us to suppose that important contracts were ratified in his name accompanied by sacrifice, communion meal and curses. The anointing of a king as a rite of consecration was certainly the occasion for a high feast day. Circum-

[1] *Gesch.*, I^3, pp. 249 ff. ($I^{5,6}$, pp. 199 ff.).

cision originally betokened the act whereby the youth was received into the fellowship of the men, and his fitness to enter into marriage was declared. The title " blood-bridegroom " and the local name " hill of the foreskin " leave no doubt about this.[1] How old this custom is can be inferred from the blood-ritual associated with it, which still bore a thoroughly demonic character.

This was the character of the religion native to Canaan that Israel found awaiting them on entering the land. How the native religion differed from and what meaning it had for Israel's own religion will be the subject of our future inquiry. We shall repeatedly have opportunity to pursue further the lines already indicated.

[1] Exod. iv. 26; Joshua v. 3.

CHAPTER II

THE GOD OF THE PATRIARCHS—MOSES

Pre-Mosaic History.

The history of Moses and of his religious foundation transports us into Egypt and into the wilderness. But according to the ancient patriarchal sagas of the Israelites those tribes from which, under Moses, Israel was to be formed, had previously dwelt in Canaan and its southern environs. Thus Israel's own tradition points us, not only for the Canaanites from whom we now pass, but also for the Israel of the pre-Mosaic period, back to Canaan and its surroundings. Is this tradition based upon mere fiction or can it claim a core of historical truth? This question is of immediate interest to us. For according to the way in which we answer it will be our picture of the religion that Moses found to exist in the Israelite tribes of his time.

The purely historical question cannot be discussed at length here. A few suggestions must suffice. So much however is clear: Israel did not rise from the soil at a stamp of Moses' foot; it must have had a previous history. The question can only be whether we to-day can still get an inkling of it. Since, then, the Old Testament records the reminiscence that patriarchal tribes of their nation migrated from the East long before,[1] since, in addition, this tradition

[1] Deut. xxvi. 5. "A wandering, that is, a vagabond (*obed*), Aramean was my father." Gen. xii. 1 ff., etc.

appears credible from internal evidence, inasmuch as migrations of closely related groups repeatedly took this route, and, further, since other independent reasons exist to show that certain groups, which appear by their names to be related to Israel, did in fact dwell in Canaan even before the time of Moses,[1] there is in reality no reason to doubt the accuracy of that tradition, at any rate in substance.

RELIGIOUS PAST.

Moreover, if the tradition of a previous history of the people in Canaan is well founded, then what it has to tell us concerning the religious past of the Hebrew fathers in Canaan will also not be spun altogether out of thin air.

As is well known, the Moses saga does not depict its hero as proposing to bring to his Egyptian brethren an entirely new God, but connects him with the "God of the Fathers". This refers to the patriarchs in Canaan.[2] At the same time the tradition alleges that the fathers worshipped strange gods on the other side of the Euphrates and again in Egypt, therefore also during the intermediate period in Canaan.[3]

What are we to think of these inconsistent traditions? We must remember that we obtained a picture of the religion of Canaan independent of the Bible. If we accept the Biblical tradition as correct, how can the picture which is given in Scripture of the religion of the Hebrew fathers in Canaan be made to fit in with the general view of religion in Canaan which we have already attained?

For the present we must take no account of the frequent mention of Yahweh in the patriarchal

[1] *Gesch.*, I[3], p. 424 (I[5, 6], p. 261). [2] Exod. iii. 6, 16 ff.
[3] Joshua xxiv. 14; cf. Gen. xxxv. 2, 4.

histories, until we have fully considered the question of the antiquity of Israel's belief in Yahweh. What remains seems to present the picture of a polytheism which reminds us in many ways of that with which we were previously confronted in Canaan and elsewhere when we discussed the names compounded with *el*. The name of the national forefather was Isra-el; his other name, Jacob, was doubtless at one time Jacob-el; one of his sons was called Joseph-el. Abraham called his sons Isma-el and Isaaq-el, for this also is the full form. For the present no ground can be brought forward for judging these names differently from similar ones which have already come to our notice. Just as in the case of Atanaḥili the *el* whom he worshipped was Nergal, so in the cases of Jacob, Joseph and Ishmael there may have been some definite *el* of unknown name, but one and the same tribal god, so far as we are dealing with members of the same tribal group. Only it should be noticed that the compound was always with *el* and not with a real name of a god. We might, of course, suspect later expurgation or assimilation of the real proper name; but just this *el* name-formation is too well attested by inscriptions for this, so that there is no reason for doubting its authenticity, and corresponding with the tradition the custom of forming names in this way must in fact have been prevalent at that time.

Again, we have to consider the question, why was it that the generic title was chosen to designate the ancestral or favourite god instead of the proper name? The answer must be the same as before, namely, that to his worshippers precisely this God appeared to be the principal God, *the* God.

THE GOD OF THE FATHERS.

According to his essential nature this God, who it seems was also named *hai*, living one, was called an *el* or *hai* of seeing, *ro'i*.[1] He was therefore a god who, because he lived, saw and looked at his worshippers, and who therein was a hearer of prayer and a helper. Moreover, he was not merely an *el* of yesterday or of to-day, but a god of ancient time, *'olam*,[2] who, as he had existed always, would also exist through all futurity and be a helper, an eternal God; at the same time his hand was not short nor straitened his power whether to help or to chastise. He was called a powerful one, an almighty one, *shaddai*.[3] Accordingly we cannot be surprised that he was even called Most High, *'elyôn*, like the Creator-god of Melkiṣedek and the God of Balaam, and therefore he towers above all the other *elim*, whose existence was not denied.[4] In the first place, so much is clear that this *el*-faith was not at all a faith in nature-beings and nature-powers. Even if the *el ro'i* showed Hagar a spring, and this perhaps seems to be connected with the ancient water-spirit of the place, as tradition knows it, it was much more. The same is true of the other titles. They are in no wise bound to nature; we do not see before us powers of nature personally conceived, to say nothing of impersonal local spirits, but a *personal* Godhead, a kindly and accessible helper, and at the same time a protector and a chastiser who towered above the limits of human time and power and indeed above other divine beings.

[1] Gen. xvi. 14; cf. Deut. xii. 7; vide *Gesch.*, I[3], pp. 364[5], 419[4] (I[5,6], pp. 215[4], 258[3]).

[2] Gen. xxi. 33; cf. Deut. xii. 7. [3] Gen. xvii. 1; Exod. vi. 3.

[4] Gen. xiv. 22, also Num. xxiv. 16; cf. *Gesch.*, I[3], p. 458 (I[5,6], p. 288).

Thus we cannot be surprised at the gentleness and kindliness with which the God, even where he is not called *el*, communicates with Abraham and his other worshippers. And even where, as in the case of Jacob at Jabbok, he still bears traces of a wild river-spirit, and thus reminds us of his ancient connexion with such,[1] here, too, he becomes a kindly being who does not part from mankind without bestowing a blessing.

From this point it is but a step to *el* being used in the patriarchal narratives of Genesis as also in the Balaam story as a true proper name. This *el* therefore was in fact reckoned God absolutely. It matters little whether the altar or the *massebah* which Jacob erected at Shechem was called " *el*, God of Israel ", or " *el* is the God of Israel ",[2] or whether the altar at Bethel was called " *el* of Bethel " or " *el* is in Bethel ".[3] In one case the seat or place where the God was revealed would be indicated, as often happens, by his own name, in the other case the name would indicate the place where the God might be found and where he belonged. Now if by translating " *el* of Bethel " we imply that the God who was present here was nothing more than a local tutelary deity or possessor, like the baal of a specific place, it is otherwise with the remaining names. But in the name " *el* is in Bethel ", which according to the context is more probable, *el* is used precisely as *elohim* or Yahweh elsewhere as a proper name for the God of Jacob. The same holds good with regard to the God of Shechem, except that here he was looked upon as the God of the people or rather as the God who personally protected Israel-Jacob. The meaning of the first proper name is thus determined. It does not, indeed, imply a monotheism, for it is to be understood in

[1] Gen. xxxii. 23 ff. [2] Gen. xxxiii. 20. [3] Gen. xxxv. 7.

the light of the second; but we have an avowal made to the God that to his worshipper he is so much the highest and worthiest among all gods that he dare regard him not only as *summus deus*, but even as God absolutely. Such is the tradition.

The Value of the Tradition.

Is this tradition credible? In the first place we may observe that the above-mentioned apparent inconsistency between the one God of the patriarchs and the plurality of gods in accordance with what we were able to establish, disappears in so far as the dominant tradition specifically recognizes the *el*-worship, and that too in the given sense. If from time to time we find references to other gods, the meaning is simply that individuals within the patriarchal circle and its immediate vicinity still paid homage to other gods.

To approach more closely the subject, we may take for our point of departure an observation in the Book of Judges. In the ninth chapter of Judges we learn that a covenant-god was worshipped in Shechem who was called *el-berîth*, or alternatively *ba'al-berîth*. The town was inhabited jointly by Canaanites and Israelites. The one called this god *el*, the others *ba'al*. In other words, the Israelites who held firmly to their religion consciously rejected *baal* as being the god of the Canaanites. Now this observation agrees with the noteworthy fact that the whole patriarchal history of Genesis is full of traces of the *el*-religion but knows nothing of baal. This is all the more remarkable as the Amarna and Egyptian texts of this period recognize baal, even a *baal ro'i*.[1] Here, therefore, baal was consciously rejected. A later expurgation is practically

[1] *Festschrift für W. Baudissin*, p. 197, and above, p. 18.

ruled out; nor can there be a question of an omission due to an idealizing motive, for in this case the name baal would certainly be all the more noticeably underlined by the Canaanites. I see therefore no other explanation than that both in the Book of Judges and in that of Genesis the records hold fast to the real fact that the worship of baal was *consciously rejected*. This view is supported by the further consideration that the worship of *el* as described in Genesis plays no part in the later period, so that a reflection of later customs cannot come into the question.

In recent times this reading of the case has indeed been controverted,[1] on the ground that the tradition of this *el*-religion, as given in the patriarchal narratives, cannot be claimed as historical, inasmuch as Genesis preserves no trace of the Amarna period. But apart from Balaam the oldest records, as we find them in the J narrative, derive from the tradition of Judah and of the southern tribes; but in the patriarchal period Judah was early pushed towards the south; the southern tribes in general did not at all live in Canaan proper but in the borderlands, so that they were not properly Egyptian subjects; at all events they were relatively untroubled by the Egyptian suzerainty. Accordingly they knew nothing of the struggles of the Amarna period. The stories of the Judges and of the conquest of the country, as we read them in the first chapter of the book of Judges and elsewhere, are apparently equally ignorant, yet there is no doubt that they contain good historical material.[2] It seems to me that the great similarity between the Biblical *el*-religion and that which we know from non-Biblical

[1] Gressmann, *Mose* (1913), p. 399.

[2] Cf. further what is said on pp. 119 f. below.

sources has considerably more weight than the silence in the book of Genesis concerning the Amarna period. Apart from the fourteenth chapter of Genesis, what should we know of the relations with Babylon from the whole section Genesis xii-l. ?

Pre-Israelites and Canaanites.

Herewith it is possible to answer the third question stated on page 40 as to the connexion between this early Hebrew *el*-religion and the remaining contemporary religion in Canaan. It is beyond doubt that the worship of that *el* played a not insignificant part among the Canaanites as also among the Babylonians. But Baal, whether as such or in connexion with the many gods of the pantheon described above, seems to have stood out as the central figure of worship. The early Hebrews, on the contrary, rejected Baal and confined themselves to *el*. They formed, therefore, as it seems, a group within the population of Canaan which differed in this point from the predominant mass of those who had been settled there for a longer period. Within these latter, however, there was yet another group, nearer to the Israelites than to their own kinsmen, a spiritual upper stratum among the Canaanites which was, at heart, in many respects strongly inclined to the *el*-faith of the early Israelites; indeed in one regard they went still further, in that they not only looked upon their god as the highest in contrast with all others, but also as the higher unity embracing all the individual gods.

Israel in Egypt.

How many of the pre-Mosaic Hebrew tribes established themselves in Canaan itself, and how many in its southern borderlands is beyond our knowledge. It is, in any case, a fact that a portion of them, more particularly Joseph, Benjamin, Simeon and Levi, were gradually driven so far southward that they chose to seek protection in the Egyptian border-land of Goshen where they remained a considerable time. It is a further fact that they were joined by tent-dwellers in the southern pastures whose manner of life essentially corresponded to the semi-nomadic form, people who were at home in those waste pastures and who stood more nearly related than they to the genuine bedouin life.

Upon these last facts rests the relative justification of the so-called bedouin theory, i.e. the notion that pre-Mosaic Israel was a group of bedouin tribes, and that they had accordingly a full polydemonistic bedouin religion. This could apply only to an insignificant percentage of those tribes out of which the Israel of Moses was composed. For this very reason we must not regard them as typical of the nation in its beginnings. We must therefore give up this idea sponsored by Robertson Smith and others; in the form which they gave to it, it is without proof and is simply based on postulates.

Hence then it is further clear that beyond what we have already learned of its *el*-religion we must not seek the religion of pre-Mosaic Israel primarily upon the field of primitive polydemonism, but on a higher plain more closely allied to the *el*-religion. The "God of the fathers"[1] of whom Moses reminded his brethren in Egypt was certainly not forgotten, but overshadowed and put into the background by others. By the "God of the fathers" we must understand

[1] Exod. iii. 6, etc.

that *el*-deity worshipped sometimes as *el 'olam*, sometimes as *el shaddai*, and sometimes exalted above all others as *el 'elyôn*. But beside this invisible *el* there was a bull deity,[1] which was certainly akin to him but removed by his pictorial representation. Hadad worshipped in the form of a bull is probably meant; he was first brought from Syria to Palestine, where he was simply called baal. The latest investigations have also revealed to us images and inscriptions of a Hathor who at that time was worshipped as *baalah* on the Sinaitic peninsula.[2] That leads us to infer a mixed religion such as admirably suits the conditions on the Sinaitic peninsula and in Goshen where the inhabitants were Canaanites, bedouin and Egyptians.

It is probable that here, too, as with the baals in Canaan the dominion of an *el* was celebrated at great stones, springs,[3] trees and on heights. It is equally certain that many of these divine beings were regarded more as impersonal spirits than as gods. There are other unmistakable traces of an ancient belief in spirits in the wilderness; even in later times we hear of a demon Asahel which dwelt there, and one of Israel's halting-places in the wilderness bore the name *'Oboth*, spirits of the dead. But such facts are to be judged precisely as similar phenomena in Canaan later on: here and there we find relics of a primitive belief which was in general superseded. Only, the wilderness by its very nature was more tenacious of such relics than cultivated land, and this is the source of an admixture of many faded and half understood conceptions.

[1] That may be surmised more particularly from the story of the Golden Calf. Exod. xxxii. 4.

[2] Cf. *Gesch.*, II^3, p. 631 (in the supplement) (II$^{6, 7}$, [1925], p. 54^3).

[3] One is reminded of the so-called "justice-spring" at Kadesh

THE CULTUS.

With regard to the cultus we may assume that it was in many ways similar to that practised in Canaan at the same time. The *asherah* must certainly have been lacking in the sparsely wooded southern country and in the wilderness. Even with respect to Canaan the *asherah* is not mentioned in Genesis, while the *massebah*, equally prized at a later time, is freely mentioned [1]—a proof that the tradition is faithfully recorded. A slaughter-table, made of earth or unhewn stone after the manner of the altar law and of the older custom followed in Canaan, did duty for an altar.[2] The slaughtered animal served as sacrifice, such as was well pleasing to God in the case of Abel. With the slaughter was connected the common meal as symbol of the communion which was sealed thereby and by the sprinkling of the blood upon those who took part in the sacrifice and upon the altar.[3] Human sacrifice, though an animal victim was early substituted, was not unknown.[4] As festivals were celebrated, the new moon in particular, so also perhaps the full moon and Sabbath, and at all events the spring full moon. At the last named, the Passover, the firstlings of the flocks were brought with propitiatory rites. We must imagine such men as Jethro as priests and seers after the fashion of the arabic *kahin*.

This was the condition in which Moses found his people when among the bedouin of the wilderness he heard the voice of a new God. Who was this

[1] Gen. xxviii. 18; Exod. xxiv. 4.
[2] Exod. xx. 24; 1 Sam. xiv. 33.
[3] Exod. xxiv. 4 ff.; cf. Gen. xv. 7 ff.
[4] Exod. xxii. 28.

Yahweh, whence came he, and what did he make out of Israel?

The Historicity of Moses.

Before we can go into these questions more fully, it is necessary to preface a few remarks concerning the problem and the sources.

Here we must presuppose that Moses and the principal facts of the tradition, the flight from Egypt, the marvellous deliverance of the people at the Red Sea, the sojourn at the oasis of Kadesh and the laying down of the law there and on Mount Sinai, all belong to strict history. But we have good grounds for doing so. For what occurred there, both in outward event and in the inward experience of souls, is from beginning to end a story quite inexplicable as the creation of the imagination of the people as a whole, and apart from a great directing genius it would for all time remain an insoluble riddle. If ever Carlyle's remark about the heroes of history is appropriate it is here. Were Moses not an historical figure, another would have to be invented; for only a man such as he could be a leader in that age; but if he existed, then he has left the mark of his spirit upon the period.

The Problem.

The problem which confronts the writer who attempts to expound the religion of Moses is to explain how the unparalleled development which the religion of Israel underwent in the course of time is intelligible in the light of its first beginnings. The ethical monotheism of the prophets must be intelligible from the foundation of the religion. It must be taken for granted, therefore, that the germ of that sublime conception of God must somehow have been already present at the beginning of the religion, particularly in the person of its founder. For nowhere in the world is personality and its peculiar power over the hearts of men so decisive as in religion. A peculiar religious genius must therefore have presided at the cradle of this unique religion. The Moses-saga gives clear expression to this in its assertion that with Moses alone Yahweh spoke face to face as a man with his friend.[1] But on the other hand we must not fail to recognize that both the older Yahweh-sagas and the religion of the people in the post-Mosaic period contain many elements which bid us beware of carelessly tricking out the figure of Moses and the picture of his religion with colours derived from the times of the great prophets. Between Moses and the great prophets a fundamental *advance* must be registered. That is one thing; on the other hand, in spite of Moses' outstanding personality there must always have been the possibility that there were in him lingering traits of primitive thought, and that in the people as a whole there must have been the possibility of their developing these into a mere religion of Nature. The task is therefore a double one: we have to make intelligible not only the advance to the fully matured monotheism of the prophets but also the falling away to the popular religion.

THE ROAD TOWARD SOLUTION.

Which way leads to our goal? In the case of the overwhelming majority of scholars more recent literary criticism has taken the position that we have no direct information about Moses. The sagas of Moses are derived from the J and E documents and are accordingly removed from the Mosaic period by

[1] Exod. xxxiii. 10; Deut. xxxiv. 10; Num. xii. 8.

centuries. Earlier forerunners of those narratives reaching further into the past are for the most part rejected. But, above all, our contemporaries, especially those of the older generation, believe that they ought to renounce the adducing of arguments from very ancient sections such as the Decalogue. Hence the course is commonly taken of trying to reconstruct the figure of Moses in the manner indicated above by arguing backwards from the post-Mosaic period. But it is obvious that here as everywhere there are limits to the method of argument from consequence to cause. It leads indeed to certain general truths and facts, but it can afford concrete traits for the picture neither of the man nor of his time.

The God of Moses. Moses the Prophet.

Söderblom has rightly described the religion of Moses as the religion of natural emotion.[1] It has long been recognized that the conception of God which is ascribed to the patriarchs in Genesis in many respects differs widely from Moses' conception of God as detailed in Exodus. The patriarchs knew a God for whom their most exalted expression was *el elyôn*, "Creator of heaven and earth", but who in other respects was represented as a kindly, quietly ruling guide and helper of his people. But now in the burning bush, amid the storms of Sinai and amid the welter of appalling natural phenomena, Moses became acquainted with a God who was himself a consuming fire and a "mighty, jealous God", one who possesses wild and terrifying traits. He was a God who smote without warning those who came too near his holy mountain and who broke forth in explosions of terrible anger.

[1] *Das Werden des Gottesglaubens* (1915), p. 309.

This God whom Moses had come to know in Egypt was a different God from the God of the fathers. This was a God who masters the soul and overpowers it with emotion. Moses was laid hold of by him and became his prophet. Just as Mohammed suddenly heard a voice which overpowered him and which drew him into the service of Allah, so Moses became aware that he was near his God who laid hold of him and constrained him into his service. Thus it was that Moses became a *prophet* not merely in name, but, what is much more important, in fact; nor was he an ecstatic prophet such as was common at a later period and was not unknown in the case of Moses' contemporaries according to the sagas, but he was a man of spiritual insight and of action. In the wilderness Moses heard God's call and was thereby constituted leader of his people. He met their great desire by giving them help in their escape from Egyptian bondage. He directed their thoughts afresh toward Canaan and the confused state of the country. He gathered together in one united whole the disunited and mutually antagonistic tribes, and he also awoke in other tribes, that still pitched their tents outside in the wilderness, the desire to join Israel in striving to reach the promised land.

Moses, the Founder of a Religion.

Now comes the crossing of the Red Sea. If any incident in the Mosaic tradition can claim to be founded upon good historical evidence it is this. We have sufficient evidence from an ancient ode indicted, according to every indication, immediately after the experience.[1] An experience such as the Exodus accomplished in spite of all its difficulties and

[1] Exod. xv. 21.

the passage through the Red Sea must have been reckoned by all who participated in it as a direct act of God. Moses was thereby authenticated in the eyes of his people. His mission as a prophet received its seal. And the common experience of need and of God's help, through which those whom he led were called to pass, only served to unite them all the more closely. The heart that had once been overwhelmed with emotion in the presence of nature was now overwhelmed by the redeeming act. The prophet became the founder of a faith, the originator of an historic religion. History became revelation, and the revelation was ratified in the experiences of history. God, so far from being a mere force within nature, became the one who ruled over nature: "he smote the Red Sea, then was it dry".[1] The nature religion had been overthrown at least in principle. Only now and then did it timidly reappear: Moses carried the magician's wand; when he raised his hand, his armies were victorious; when he let it sink, they became powerless. These and other traits pertain to the seer and priest of ancient times. They were to be found in Moses, but they were not the determining elements; they only serve to prove that the picture fits the framework of the age, and that we are not dealing with a shadow but with a human being of flesh and blood.

The God of the Moral Will.

Moses came with his people to Kadesh and to the Mount of God. Here justice and conscience won their victory in his religion. God was a God of moral will.

From of old the tribes of the peninsula may have met together in the oasis of Kadesh at the "justice-

[1] Ps. cvi. 9.

spring ", *'en mishpat,* to seek justice and to settle their disputes. The spring and its environment were sacred territory; this is self-evident in the case of the spring and is proven so by the name *qadesh* in the case of the neighbourhood.

The *el* of Kadesh then will have ruled and his oracle have spoken here. But this is only conceivable if the tribes which gathered laid aside their feuds during their sojourn here. Thus Kadesh naturally became the place of covenant, and its god, like the *el* of Shechem, became the covenant god, for it is inconceivable that gatherings of the tribes for such purposes should take place without the celebration of festal rites under the protection of the deity. But the Israel that was in Egypt appears already to have belonged to this confederation, which would seem to have been established by the Levites who were probably an ancient Leah tribe; and Moses, also a Levite, came to the priests of Kadesh who initiated him into the worship of their *el* of Kadesh, that perhaps already bore the name Yahweh. Moreover the feast which took Israel three days' journey into the wilderness was probably a feast of this *el* of Kadesh; probably the pastoral feast of the passover which was designed to protect the flocks from the evil powers.

We learn from an especially reliable tradition that here in Kadesh Moses gave the people " statutes and ordinances ", *hoq umishpat.*[1] It was fitting immediately to write down these statutes as words " of the covenant ", therefore as a charter of the covenant, and with these as its basis the covenant was solemnly concluded.[2] Thus the relationship of Israel to its God was that of a contract, a solemn ethical obligation

[1] Exod. xv. 25. [2] Exod. xxiv. 3 ff.; Joshua xxiv. 1–25 ff.

to do his will. But Moses himself hereby became *law-giver*, though not of course in the sense that he gave them the later so-called Mosaic Law, or that he imparted it as a completed code; for everybody knows that this was the work of centuries of constant development. He was law-giver rather in the sense that he gave his people norms of conduct and controlled in the name of the deity the decisions given at the sanctuary. Both elements, *jus* and *fas*, bore the name *torah*, divine instruction.

THE LAW.

We have to ask what kind of statutes these were. Their chief clause ran as follows: "I, Yahweh, am thy God, thou shalt have none other gods beside me." That represents the exacting exclusiveness, the consuming jealousy of the God who had revealed himself to Moses. He was a God of fearful "holiness"; all that did not belong to him was an abomination to him, it was *tabu* in respect of him; and at the same time all that belonged to him was also *tabu* as partaking to some extent in his "holiness". Moreover to approach him was dangerous in the highest degree, and his severity was inexorable. Thus it was that every pictorial representation of him was forbidden. There are other cases when it was thought dangerous to touch the god's images, but here it was sacrilege even to make any image of the God. Not that images were unknown, for they were to be seen in Egypt and in the quarries of the Sinaitic peninsula and elsewhere, although the Canaanites but rarely made use of them. Nor was it as if there was no man in Israel capable of constructing an image of God. Although the artistic faculty was but scantily developed, yet it was always sufficient for a simple image. Rather, just as the name of God was considered too high for daily use, so he himself was thought to be too high and unapproachable to be represented by human hands, and, further, because he was God of history and his worship was based upon soul-experiences, he was a spiritual God raised above nature and history. If at first people did not understand this motive, they soon came to interpret the repudiation of images in this sense. Everything therefore related to customs or edible animals used in connexion with "other gods", whatever name they bore, was *unclean*. And, on the other hand, Yahweh's day must be kept sacred as also everything done in honour of Yahweh, and, above all, waging war with nations foreign to them and their God. The servants of other gods were Yahweh's enemies, wars against them were holy wars and a service to Yahweh. The battle-cry resounded in his name. He himself with his heavenly hosts went before Israel's earthly armies as their supreme war-lord; thus he led them into Canaan.

Here we can see a remarkable coalescence of two ideas. The God of the fathers whose place was taken by Yahweh was as *el 'elyôn* closely related to the "lord of the gods" of the ancient Canaanites, and as *el* simply he was the God who, to those who accepted him, seemed the most worthy and therefore the highest of all. The Yahweh of Moses took all that over. The God of the fathers revived but in an entirely new guise. Instead of an unadorned statement of truth we find a stern command, instead of the calm word of the Most High we find a jealous exclusiveness. Acknowledgement and quiet worship became a passion of emotion. But the fruitful influence of the patriarchs is unmistakable. Indeed, it is not impossible that in the unique claims of Yahweh we see the working out of that unity in multiplicity which had been recognized by the few in Canaan. At all events, it would seem certain that the inheritance from the patriarchs co-operated in the spiritualizing of the savage and terrible *tabu* of the wilderness-god of Sinai.

The Cultus. The Ark and the Tent.

As is the case with all ancient religions, the worship of this God was celebrated essentially by means of the cultus; with this therefore the statutes were necessarily concerned. The tent of revelation, called the Tabernacle, containing the sacred ark was according to the tradition the real sanctuary of Moses' time. Now there is no doubt that the detailed description of the tent which has been handed down to us in the Priestly Code belongs to a much later date. Consequently in recent times critics have to their satisfaction controverted the tradition of Moses' sacred tent, but without justification. Not only have we too many parallel cases among other Semitic peoples such as the Carthaginians and Arabians, amongst whom such a portable tent played a great part,[1] partly as a palladium of war, and partly as the place where the god revealed himself, but also the tent is too firmly established in the Biblical tradition to admit of its being simply put on one side.[2] In addition, the fact of the wandering in the wilderness of itself authenticates the tradition of a portable tabernacle. Our only real question can be whether the tent should be considered as being in itself an

[1] Rich. Hartmann in *Zeitschr. f. Alttest. Wiss.* 37 (1917–1918), pp. 217 ff.

[2] Exod, xxxiii. 7 ff.; 2 Sam. vii. 1 ff.

empty dwelling-place of the invisible God or as existing only in connexion with the sacred ark and as its abiding place. This latter is the view commonly held by those who accept the tradition about the tent. Then the ark is usually taken to be a throne for the god after the fashion of the elsewhere well attested throne-shrines. In that case the ark would be the place of the presence of Yahweh of whom it is often said that he was "enthroned above the cherubim" (the ark).

While so much appears to speak for this conception, yet against it is constantly raised the objection deserving careful attention that an ark, or more accurately a chest or shrine, *'aron*, manifestly could not properly be described as a throne. Consequently many questions remain unanswered. It cannot be claimed with perfect certainty that the ark originally belonged to the tent, nor indeed that like the tent it derives from Moses himself. It may also have been a chest for the taking of lots or for use in processions, existing independently of the tent. Others have thought of the chest in which the bones of Joseph were brought to Canaan. The ark in the above sense may not have been the only one of its kind in existence. It may be that every great sanctuary, at least in Palestine, possessed such an one.[1]

[1] W. R. Arnold, *Ephod and Ark*, Cambridge, Mass., 1917. Gressmann, *Die Lade Jahwes*, 1920. There is no evidence for G.'s explanation of the ark as the receptacle for an image. That could only be the case on the supposition that it was a pre-Israelite chest used in processions taken over from the Canaanites or Midianites and stripped of its original image. But there is nothing to show that under David and Solomon an image of Baal and Astarte was carried round in the ark; certainly this is not indicated by Solomon's oracle about the Temple, where Gressmann's insertion of Baal only ruins both the form and content of the passage. See also p. 84.

ORACLE. PRIESTS.

According to reliable tradition the "inquiry of God" played an important part in connexion with the tent in the Mosaic period.[1] We may therefore concede an essential place in it to the Yahweh-oracle. In later times also the oracle was closely bound up with the ark and with the priesthood. The common means of giving the oracle was the *ephod*, a wrap or bag concealing the sacred *lots*; these latter bore the name *urim* and *thummim* and consisted of two sticks or stones which replied with Yes or No to a question addressed to Yahweh.[2] Many scholars also suppose that in close connexion with the oracle tent stood the *teraphim*, an oracular device which was perhaps much more ancient and which according to tradition had been introduced from Aram (it can scarcely have been the image of a household god).[3] On the other hand, it is hazardous to argue from the story of the brazen serpent to a snake-cult in the time of Moses. Doubtless it developed gradually at a later period. But it seems certain that Moses' rod, which according to the legend was changed into a serpent, must have been some sort of serpent-engirdled magician's wand[4] comparable to the staff of Asclepius, just as elsewhere Yahweh also appears as a god of healing.[5]

It seems doubtful whether Moses published new regulations or rather maintained ancient customs concerning sacrifice and the altar. The custom of circumcision does not derive from him. It appears

[1] Exod. xxxiii. 7; cf. xviii. 13 ff.

[2] 1 Sam. xiv. 41 ff.

[3] Cf. the way it is brought into connexion with the ephod, Judges xvii. 5, xviii. 14 ff.; Hos. iii. 4.

[4] Exod. iv. 3.

[5] Exod. xv. 22. Yahweh the physician.

to have only fallen into disuse in Egypt, and now to have been resumed afresh.[1] The same is true of the Passover and the Sabbath. Only, in the case of the former, stress was laid upon the redemption of the human first-born, and of the latter it should be observed that it is the only part of the cultus of which mention is made in the ethical decalogue of Exodus xx. From this we may conclude that it was considered the principal feast of Moses' day. Or may we perhaps infer that the Sabbath was instituted by Moses himself? Moses was pre-eminently priest. The control of the Yahweh oracle and the ministry of the altar belonged to him, but he needed assistants. For this purpose he chose the *Levites*, probably his fellow-tribesmen, who from thenceforth claimed an especial right to the priesthood. For a long time they had to share this privilege with the heads of families and of tribes, but no one disputed their long-standing and especial status as the servants of Yahweh; for this reason also they possessed no tribal territory, but wandered about among the tribes and tendered their offices.[2]

Law and Ethics.

The third type of commandment which Moses gave, apart from questions of religion and worship, was designed to regulate law and morality. The view has often been propounded that such clauses as we find in the second half of the familiar decalogue are not to be expected till the period of the prophets, that ancient Israel was limited to cultus-regulations alone. This viewpoint suffers from a twofold error: it overlooks the fact that long before the time of Moses other peoples closely akin to Israel had ordained

[1] Exod. iv. 24–26; Joshua v. 1 ff. [2] Judges xvii. 7 ff.

similar purely ethical statutes [1]; but above all, and this is a much more fatal error, the Israel of Moses' day, according to all that we may take for granted of its past and its environment, was no longer at the absolutely *primitive* stage.

There is therefore no occasion to dispute Moses' authorship of these passages, and they formed very naturally the ground-work both for the ethical requirements upon which he based his religious foundation and at the same time for the legal code the fundamental principles and forms of which he laid down. Those legal statutes in closest connexion with the sacred constitution are set forth for us in the so-called Book of the Covenant. We have it in two redactions.[2] This, however, is not the place in which to treat of them more fully, but my own well-considered conviction is that we may without hesitation ascribe to Moses the initial stimulus to this customary law, which was undoubtedly at first transmitted orally, together with many of its clauses.

What gives special importance to these laws is that law and religion, indeed, ethics and religion, are brought into most intimate connexion. Both were logically and clearly put under the protection of the Deity. Yahweh became a God of the moral will, the Yahweh-religion became an *ethical religion.* Its worship was not merely monolatry, the service of one God only, but its conception of God, although not as yet the ethical monotheism of the prophets, was nevertheless a national and ethical henotheism. Yahweh was not yet for Moses as for his great successors a world-God, but certainly he was an

[1] For Egypt and Babylon, see *Gesch.*, I³, p. 654 (I⁵·⁶, p. 445); also a corresponding reference to primitive peoples, following Söderblom.

[2] Exod. xxi.–xxiii. and Exod. xxxiv. 11 ff.

ethical national God, lord and protector of an ethical national order, and the way was prepared for ethical monotheism.

Origin of Yahweh.

This was the Yahweh of Moses. What was his origin ?

We know what was understood by the name Yahweh in Israel at the beginning of the first millennium. He was described as the one who took a living part, that is, as the living helper, very much as the *'el ro'i* and *el 'olam* of the patriarchs was accounted a living and enduring helper and answerer of prayer. Thus his name was used in taking oaths. We cannot decide with certainty what thoughts were originally and in Moses' time connected with the name Yahweh. Correspondingly we also do not know the precise origin of Yahweh.[1] Israelite tradition lays stress on the fact that the worship of Yahweh goes back to Moses as its founder; it claims that before his time God was known as *el shaddai*.[2] This is probably accurate. True, attempts have been made and are constantly being made to prove that the name Yahweh, especially in its abbreviated form, Yau, was already current long before the time of Moses outside Israel. But this is incorrect. If in ancient times abroad, somewhere far east and north, there was a god of similar name, then it is much more likely to be a question of accidental similarity of sound than of identity. When, however, it is a question of later periods, then in view of the high prestige enjoyed by Israel and its God after the time of David and Solomon, we can easily assume borrow-

[1] Exod. iii. 14. So should we interpret *ehyè asher ehyè*.

[2] Exod. iii. 11 ff., vi. 1 ff.

ing from Israel.[1] On the other hand, it is a highly instructive fact that in Israel itself the name Joshua was the first to be definitely compounded with that of Yahweh, and that from that time onwards such names are found continually.

Yahweh a God of the Kenites?

From this we infer that Yahweh was neither borrowed from distant foreign countries, nor was he at home in Israel from antiquity. His naturalization in Israel was the work of Moses and a part of his religious foundation. Now the circumstance that Moses came to know him in the wilderness in the territory of the Midianite Kènites together with his close connexion with their priests[2] has led recent scholars to suppose that Yahweh was originally the God of the Kenites, and that Moses adopted him and his worship from that source. Concerning this we may observe that if Moses did not coin the name himself, but, as is quite possible, merely adopted it, there is still no proof of specifically Kenite origin. He might just as well have been the God of one particular Israelite tribe, perhaps of Moses' own family,[3] although, it is true, the narrative of the burning bush presupposes that up to that time the name was unknown to Moses. From Jethro's visit to Moses we may only conclude that Moses received a stimulus for the administration of justice from him, but not for worship. Beyond this all belongs to the sphere of imagination.

The whole question is, however, of comparatively little consequence, for from whatever quarter Moses may have received the name, it was only the name

[1] This applies to the North Syrian royal names of the eighth century, Iaubidi and Azriyau. Cf. *Gesch.*, I³, p. 586*n* (I⁵·⁶ p. 387*n*).

[2] Exod. xviii; Judges iv. 11. (Hobab the Kenite.)

[3] Exod. iii. 6. (God of thy father.)

that he took; its connotation is due to him. All depends on what Moses made of this God whom he may have adopted from somewhere, or, more accurately, what conception of the deity he gained through this God. It is beyond question that the God of Moses still bore traces of local influences from the wilderness, from whatever wilderness tribes they may have been derived. Reminiscences of the terrible nature-God, flashing fire, are everywhere still discernible. But that was only the original given element in Moses' conception of God, and this had been vanquished by the remembrance of the God of his fathers; this was not the God himself. He was a great ethical Being, and, again, it was precisely this which the Kenite god was not.

CHAPTER III

SETTLING IN THE COUNTRY—YAHWEH AND BAAL

TWO RELIGIONS.

We have just made the observation that Moses' conception of God had a twofold aspect. On the one hand Yahweh was a great moral God who protected the moral order in Israel. He was indeed a God unique, supreme, holding himself jealously apart from all other gods. But this he was in a manner which betrays the fact that there were still connected with him traits deriving from an ancient, terrible nature-deity of the wilderness.

This is a guide for us: it was inevitable that these two sides in the nature of Yahweh, which in a measure probably Moses' personality alone was able to combine, should after his death fall asunder. Each aspect found some among the people to adopt and approve it, and each group strove to conquer within their circle. Just as later the state broke up into two states, or just as here and there in many churches to-day two modes of the faith live side by side, so it was in this case also. There were two fundamentally different religions: the popular religion and the higher religion, the one opposed to the other, but having this in common that they both confessed the name of Yahweh.

The cleavage might also have taken place had Israel remained in the wilderness. Only it would have manifested itself quite differently than in Canaan, namely, along the lines just indicated. Moreover the wilderness sagas show traces enough which indicate this and may well be taken for reminiscences of this situation. I have in mind the golden calf and Baal Peor. But in the country upon which Israel had now set foot the cleavage became inevitable, and here also it manifested itself in a particular form. To be sure, it was not Sinai's nature-god of the storm who held sway there, but rather nature-religion in a form which was especially dangerous to Israel as they issued from the wilderness, namely, as an indigenous religion. The Israelites were strangers in Canaan, whether they had become such or had always been such ; how then were they to find their bearings in the country without the aid of the inhabitants who for centuries had dwelt there ?

New Problems for Israel.

The period which followed immediately upon the death of Moses had brought Israel into the country. It was not as if they had now all at once become sole possessors and undisputed masters of the land, yet so that they acquired firm control of certain districts, particularly in the mountains ; elsewhere, as for instance in the towns, they shared possession with those who had previously been lords of the land.[1] The entry into the country involved the acquisition of numerous arts. For the present and indeed for a considerable time a part of the people continued to live their former nomadic life, but they were in the minority. The remaining portion had much to learn.

[1] See Kittel, *Gesch.*, II[3], (1917), p. 59 (II[6, 7], [1925], p. 5).

The very act of settlement itself brought problems. On the level ground a village with firm clay huts or stone houses took the place of an encampment. Within the towns in addition to houses were the fortifications with encircling walls or ramparts, moats and towers. Apart from agriculture and horticulture the inhabitants lived by industry and trade. All these things had to be learnt. For the learning of them the conquerors, so far as they were conquerors, were in many ways dependent upon the good-will of the natives. Thus they naturally came very much under their influence; other influences were added.

The Canaanites of that time had already attained to a comparatively high standard of culture, so that the Israelites often had occasion to look to them for guidance. Egyptian merchants and garrisons in the land brought into it the products of Egyptian industrial enterprise, and the large commercial cities along the coast introduced all kinds of valuable merchandise, and themselves produced costly materials and fabrics.[1] Archives attest an extensive use of writing; many foreign stories and myths spread throughout the land.[2]

Of all this Israel in the wilderness had little or nothing, at any rate no more than the rudiments. Elsewhere I have shown approximately how we should suppose the palace or governor's house of Gideon or Abimelech to have been furnished.[3] Whatever was to be seen of art or of artistic equipment in the house of a Hebrew of distinction will have been produced by the Canaanites directly or have been acquired through their commercial enterprise. Simi-

[1] See *Gesch.*, I3, pp. 183 ff. (I5, 6, pp. 147 ff.); II3, p. 115 (II6, 7, pp. 49 f.).

[2] Ibid., I3, pp. 195 ff. (I5, 6, pp. 156 f.); II3, pp. 120, 631 (II6, 7, pp. 53 f.).

[3] Ibid., II3, p. 115[1] and [3] (II6, 7, p. 49[1] and [3])

larly the rare spoils of cloth, for which in the days of Debora the women of Sisera so eagerly waited, were the products of Sidon. Even in these matters the Canaanites were the schoolmasters of Israel and often enough doubtless their admired models. Yet this circumstance did not necessarily involve any serious religious consequences, but in the province of agriculture they were of necessity bound to follow. The life of a peasant in Canaan had to be learnt. Cattle farming is not self-evident to the sheep-herder. Insomuch as sheep, goats and cattle must be driven to pasture, a knowledge of the pasturage and of the peculiarities differentiating it from that in the wilderness had to be gained. In particular, farming in the oasis of the desert was quite a different matter from that on the heights and on the terraces of Judah or on the fields and slopes of Benjamin and Ephraim. The planting and enclosure of gardens and the cultivation in them of the native fruits, the vine, the fig and the olive trees, are not matters which are obvious to those who come from the wilderness. First the ground had to be carefully studied, its secrets diligently sought out; care must be taken of wind and weather; dew, rain and springs must be the objects of study.

Influence of the Baal Religion.

But all this only took the Israelite half-way; he must further penetrate all the other secrets which soil, climate and springs conceal; he must discover the supreme secret wherein consists the prosperity of the crops and which is controlled by one higher than man. It is the help which comes from above, the blessing of the deity. The Canaanites had been in possession of this secret from of yore. Here if anywhere in the world this people's religion, as we saw it in Chapter I, was accommodated to the land which they cultivated and suited to the land's peculiarities. The baals of Canaan were the possessors of the springs, trees and fields of the country, the dispensers of its gifts, the protectors and increasers of its flocks. It was they who dispensed to the peasant " bread and water, wool and flax, oil and drink ".[1] Every field had its baal, so also had every village and town. Upon the village high places, at the sacrificial stones, " upon every high hill and under every green tree ", offerings were gratefully brought by the pious in honour of the baal who was the dispenser of fruitfulness.[2] On days of festival and of sacrifice the jubilant praises of the giver of fruitfulness to field and flock resounded far and wide. How could it be but that those, who with wonder were busy learning the secrets of the soil and of the arts of cultivating it, did not disdain to learn from the inhabitants the last secret concerning the help which came from beyond human power and skill. Many frankly joined in going to the baals on the high places and did homage to them. These were lost to Israel. Others went, but, when there, thought of Yahweh. They knew of no other way of ensuring the fertilizing power of the earth and the fruitfulness of the flocks. They consciously remained loyal to Yahweh, but they worshipped him under the forms of baal-worship. They paid homage to baal and meant Yahweh. Thus Yahweh worshippers could call themselves after baal without giving up Yahweh. Gideon bore the name Jerubbaal, and in Shechem there was probably a Jobaal, who in his name, " Yahweh is Baal ", exactly represented this fusion of the two.[3]

[1] Hos. ii. 7. [2] Deut. xii. 2 ; 1 Kings xiv. 23.
[3] See Judges ix. 26 and the Author's *Bibl. Heb.* ad loc.

Together with the people of baal they went to the high places and venerated the massebahs and asherahs; with them they joined in their festivals and followed their customs.

THE GREAT GAP.

Was this inevitable? Up to a certain point this association in the friendly common life of neighbours may have been unavoidable. The adoption of such indigenous feasts as the three great annual festivals Moses might well have commanded, as indeed the Book of the Covenant traces them back to his institution,[1] but many other things certainly not. Accordingly those who felt themselves to be his heirs in a special sense repudiated them. The prophets would have nothing to do with massebahs and asherahs and much that was connected with them. They also stood aloof from other things which Moses probably allowed—undoubtedly in the assurance that they were following him in going beyond him.

At this point the removal of Moses was fateful for his people. Often in history decisive moments of a people's life depend upon a single leader or on a few men. If they are removed, the gap they leave first makes clear how great the loss is. So it was in this case. Hitherto Yahweh had not been worshipped in Canaan; he came from the desert. The genius of Moses would have discovered a form of transition for Yahweh into the new country; creative power was lacking in the new generation; hence Moses' work was in danger of going to pieces. His death had made a gap which no one left was able to fill.

[1] Exod. xxiii. 14 ff., xxxiv. 18 ff., 23.

THE POPULAR RELIGION.

Those who take a short-sighted view of the period succeeding the death of Moses always take it amiss when it is described as a retrograde period. This was the fact. And as the time was retrograde in respect of political life, so probably also in the sphere of religion. The nature-elements in Yahweh, instead of being overcome by the higher aspect of his being, were associated in Canaan with the nature-elements in baal and threatened to submerge the moral and spiritual elements. Thus it was that the POPULAR RELIGION came into being. This was the situation in Israel against which the later prophets waged so fierce a war; for they saw that the exalted God of Moses was in danger of being degraded into a mere local nature-power. This then was the root cause of the appearance of the great prophets and of their frequent opposition to their nation.

Under these circumstances the first thing was the joint use of the places of sacrifice and prayer with the Canaanites. The "high places" of such localities as Gibeah, Ramah, Mispah, Peniel, Gilgal, Bethel, Beersheba and many others at the conquest were either simply handed over to Israel or shared between the Israelites and the Canaanites. In Shechem, where the two lived side by side, there was, according to Judges ix., a temple to baal of the covenant. To this god Israel also paid homage, only they called him *el* of the covenant; undoubtedly they meant Yahweh by this. Sacred trees, springs and stones, including also the massebahs, were to be found everywhere; frequently also, as in Ophrah, the asherah.[1] Here and there altars also were added; these in the course of

[1] Judges vi. 25 ff.

time and with the adoption of burnt sacrifice became progressively more frequent. At the more important sanctuaries they must have been numerous to suffice for the multitude of worshippers. There were even to be found eating-rooms and halls and special cooks for the sacrificial meals.[1] In Shechem and Shiloh we find special temples; so it will long have been among the Canaanites, and so these were taken over by the Israelites—the only difference being that now Yahweh reigned instead of Baal. Wealthy people had their own sanctuaries, shrines such as that of Micah on the heights of Ephraim and that of Gideon's father at Ophrah.[2]

After Solomon in the northern kingdom Bethel and Dan played an important rôle, the latter as a royal sanctuary.[3] In spring the beginning of harvest was celebrated at the feast of the Mazzoth. By those who had not yet gone over to agriculture the Passover, the ancient feast of the desert, will have been preferred. This was also the time to offer the firstlings of the flocks.[4] In summer the wheat harvest was celebrated by festivities and in autumn the ingathering of the vintage. Hilarious meals, festive jubilation and dancing were not lacking.

Absalom invited two hundred guests to his sacrifice in Hebron, and Solomon invited many more in Gibeon and Jerusalem.[5] At the great temples festive garments were placed at the disposal of those who participated in the celebrations.[6] The crowds appeared in the forecourt, and at the altar stood the priests. The people joined in the singing and the prayer. Those who were especially moved (by

[1] 1 Sam. ix. 22, I[9], p. 18. [2] Judges xvii. 5 and vi. 25.
[3] 1 Kings xii. 29; Amos vii. 13. [4] 1 Sam. x. 3.
[5] 2 Sam. xv. 11; 1 Kings iii. 4, viii. 1 ff., 5. [6] 2 Kings x. 22.

the divine spirit) would recite a song, perhaps to the accompaniment of the zither; others would give an address, especially priests and those under the prophetic inspiration.[1] All this served to extol Yahweh and to heighten the feeling of communion with him. But the further the identification of Yahweh with Baal was developed, the more the orgiastic traits of the baal-worship came into prominence. Wine must on occasion have flowed in streams.[2] Therewith the lower instincts were let loose, and all the perversions of the baal-religion were inevitably introduced.

The Ephod and the Ark.

Those circles in Israel to whom the nature-elements in the Mosaic Yahweh had appeared of religious value, found here flesh of their flesh. The later account reproaches Gideon for having set up an ephod.[3] This may rightly reflect the opinion of many who saw more deeply, but it was not so with the majority. The ephod seems to have been an heirloom from the Mosaic period; this Gideon could claim. In post-Mosaic times it stood in very close connexion with the ark, which was indeed the ancient desert-sanctuary of the Joseph tribes. So the ark itself came to be involved in the half-Canaanite cultus. It had long had a tent to house it, as it had had in the period of the desert wanderings; in this it would appear to have been moved about from place to

[1] Cf. the various addresses with which the prophetical books are interlarded and which presuppose the divine service, e.g. Isa. i. 10 ff., xxviii. 7 ff.; Amos vii. 1 ff., 10 ff.; similarly many Psalms or sections of Psalms, which must derive from ancient and perhaps even pre-Israelite cultus practices. 1 Sam. ii. 1 ff.; Ps. xcv. 6 ff. (also my commentary ad. loc.), etc.

[2] Isa. xxviii. 7 f.; Sam. i. 14 f.

[3] Judges viii. 27*b*.

place in Canaan among the tribes according to need.[1] It was accompanied by its priests (from an early date these were mostly Levites) with the ephod, very likely also with the teraphim, which is commonly mentioned with the ephod, and certainly with the sacred lot, the urim and thummim. For a time it had a solid temple, a new visible concession to certain customs of the country. That was in Shiloh under Eli and his sons. How far in that period Yahweh had sunk to the level of a demonic being without the exalted elements of the God of Moses is made evident by certain scenes thoroughly reminiscent of the fierce and terrible tabu of the jealous Mosaic God.[2] At a later date David gave it back a tent, perhaps the same tent that had belonged to it prior to the time of Eli.[3] In doing this he followed a custom that was still alive in Judah of which we shall hear; besides this he won the allegiance of the non-Judean elements in his kingdom to the new capital by means of the ark which was particularly estimated in Ephraim. Inasmuch as the ark even in early days occasionally bore the name of "the ark of the covenant",[4] we may perhaps see an ancient connexion between it and the covenant-god of Shechem.

Divine Images.

The ephod is often taken for a divine image, probably without justification; but even if this is not the case, it is nevertheless certain that at this time the popular religion made use of divine images; there

[1] 2 Sam. vii. 6 f.; cf. v. 2.

[2] 1 Sam. vi. 19; 2 Sam. vi. 6 ff.

[3] 2 Sam. vi. 17.

[4] 2 Sam. xv. 24. At a later period this name seems to have come into general use, so that it was then in many places inserted into the ancient texts.

are traces even in the Mosaic tradition, that occasionally the calf-image sought to displace the imageless Yahweh.[1]

In Gilgal, on the banks of the Jordan, there were carved images to which the Benjamites repaired to consult the oracles.[2] What these images represented we do not know. In Dan on the northern boundary of Palestine and at Bethel also, at any rate from the time of Jeroboam I, if not earlier, there stood a bull-image.[3] Under this form Yahweh was worshipped in a similar manner as Hadad-Ramman, the Aramean weather-god, who in Palestine will have held a position somewhat similar to that of Baal. As god of the weather he was at the same time protector of vegetation and of fertility. Up to this time we have no proof of a human image of Yahweh; one, which was published years ago by Dalman, is a palpable forgery.[4]

It is possible that such an image stood in the house of that Micah of whom we read in Judges xvii. who dwelt on the hills of Ephraim. But even here the greater probability is that it was a bull-image. As there were enough people who, after the pattern of this Micah or Gideon's father in Ophrah, built for themselves on their own ground and estate a small shrine, a sort of private chapel, so it is certain that there must have been divine images of all sorts in the hands and houses of countless individuals, so much so that Isaiah could still complain, " their country is full of idols, they bow down to the work of their hands ".[5]

[1] Exod. xxxii., the Golden " Calf ".

[2] Judges iii. 19.

[3] 1 Kings xii. 29.

[4] *Palästin. Jahrbuch des ev. Inst. f. Altert-kunde*, II 1907, 44 ff.; cf. my *Gesch.*, II[3], p. 255[2] (II[6, 7], p. 157[1]).

[5] Isa. ii. 8, 18, 20.

But here, as the excavations suggest, we have to do for the most part with little images in the form of amulets or of the value of talismans which served all kinds of witchcraft and superstitious customs. Besides Astarte-images, for the most part of noticeably foreign type, we find mostly strange, predominantly Egyptian deities. As far as we know, however, such images were not introduced into the public cultus, unless the "abominable thing" which king Asa's mother introduced into the temple at Jerusalem for a short time was such an image[1]; but this is not likely, if only for the reason that it was probably something worse.

MAGIC.

Images of Baal are once mentioned.[2] Like those of Yahweh they seem to have been rare, except so far as the bull-image was a symbolization of Baal. Nor do we find a Yahweh image in the brazen serpent which dates back to Moses and was still cultivated in the time of King Hezekiah,[3] though hardly in the temple, but rather at the serpent-stone and dragon-spring in the Valley of Kidron, close to which David's tent was pitched.[4] Never was Yahweh represented as a Serpent as he was at times as a Rock or a Bull. It was simply the badge of Yahweh which designated him the God of healing. Serpents were in his service as health-producing creatures. The serpent on Moses' rod expresses this. Whoever made a sacrifice before the serpent, avowed Yahweh as the Healer. But just as the saint comes to be worshipped instead of God, so many people among the masses could misuse the serpent on the rod and take it for the God himself.

[1] 1 Kings xv. 13.
[2] 1 Kings xi. 18.
[3] Num. xxi. 9; 2 Kings xviii. 4.
[4] 1 Kings i. 39.

Although the ephod and teraphim, especially when, as happened in the course of time, they were separated from the ark,[1] and still more the brazen serpent and all the little images and amulets belonged to the province of magic, we find elsewhere, also, many traces of magic. The whole oracular system of Israel differed very little from that of other nations. Men believed in evil forebodings and sought to obviate them.[2] They heard Yahweh's voice in the rustling of the trees.[3] They summoned the spirits of the dead to learn the future from them.[4] There were many "wise persons" and "mutterers" who had at their disposal particular secrets which they secretly imparted.[5] They did not even shun human sacrifice to propitiate the spirits under ground.[6] As in ancient Canaan they manifestly still felt themselves surrounded on every side by spirits, and men's minds were held in thrall by anxious superstitions. People were not lacking who knew how to turn these and other elements in the popular religion to their own advantage. Among the class of holy persons whose reputation with the masses rested upon their valuation as being possessed by some spirit or even by Yahweh himself, a very considerable number lived upon the favour and so naturally upon the superstitions of the people. Their speech was calculated to gratify their hearers rather than to reprove their superstitions, and "they declared war on any who put nothing in their mouths".[7] Amos was ashamed of being mistaken for one of them.[8]

[1] 1 Sam. xxiii. 3, 6, xxx. 7, xix. 13, 16.
[2] Gen. xv. 11.
[3] 2 Sam. v. 24.
[4] 1 Sam. xxviii. 7 ff.; Isa. viii. 19.
[5] Isa. viii. 19.
[6] 1 Kings xvi. 34.
[7] Mic. iii. 5.
[8] Amos vii. 14.

YAHWEH HIMSELF.

Under these circumstances it was natural that Yahweh himself should have been transformed. How closely he approximated to the Baal of the Canaanites is best indicated by the names in high favour to the time of David, and then, as we learn from the potsherds of Samaria, again in vogue under Ahab,[1] such as Jerubbaal, Eshbaal, Meribaal, Beeliadah and Jobaal. Essentially this Yahweh differed little from the Baal of Palestine or Chemosh of Moab or Milcom of Ammon, as the principle *cuius regio eius religio* was incidentally applied to him. His sphere was Canaan; the world outside was the empire of other gods.[2] Accordingly in respect of his power, his knowledge and his other attributes Yahweh was subjected to great limitations. He was neither almighty nor omni-present nor all-wise. He shared the government of the world with the other gods, and, quite contrary to the Mosaic exclusiveness, he was put virtually on a level with them.[3] He had his dwelling-place in the land at the sacred spots, particularly with the ark,[4] but also outside upon Horeb or Sinai, and that too in such a way that he permanently abode in the latter and only issued forth to visit the former on special occasions.[5] In the latter idea we glimpse the memory of the God of Sinai; in the former he is just like one of the local baals. But even where he was regarded as God of heaven, he must descend before he can see what mankind was doing and whether that which reached him as rumour or appeal was true.[6]

[1] *Gesch.*, II^3, pp. 385, 374^2 (II^{6,7}, pp. 245, 236^6, 447).

[2] 1 Sam. xxvi. 19; Judges xi. 24. Cf. *Gesch.*, II^3, p. 463^1 (II^{6,7}, p. 307^1).

[3] Judges xi. 24.

[4] 1 Sam. iv. 4 ff.

[5] Judges v. 4 f.; Deut. xxxiii. 2; 1 Kings xix. 8 ff.

[6] Gen. iii. 8, xi. 5, xviii. 20 f. (the Fall, the building of the Tower, Sodom).

Yahweh and Morality.

Moreover he was not above caprice and passion, and even had fits of anxiety and of envy.[1] Indeed he was provoked to anger without visible reason, especially when provoked by a curse uttered by man.[2] He was, moreover, capable of inciting man to do evil or of deceiving him by a lying spirit in order to be able to punish him subsequently.[3] From his ark, if it was too nearly approached, he would unexpectedly send forth fearful retribution.[4] In sum his connexion with morality was exceedingly loose. He was beyond good and evil. His relationship to Israel corresponded with this. He was the God of this people, and it was his duty as such to stand on their side. The popular religion knew nothing of ethical conditions in this connexion. It was not so much a sense of moral duty which prompted the people to bring their sacrifices and offerings as a sense of prudence; the deity must be kept in good humour. The cultus was a performance, *opus operatum*,[5] along the lines of the principle *do ut des*. Wrong-doing was more an offence against good form than sin against Yahweh[6]: " such things are not done in Israel ".

The Higher Religion.

Meanwhile alongside of this broad stream of Canaanized life and thought in Israel, which reduced Yahweh half or three quarters to the level of baal, there was another. Never in history have the great masses of the people been in sympathy with that which corresponds with the finer insight and above all with

[1] Gen. iii. 22, xi. 6.
[2] 1 Sam. xxvi. 19.
[3] 2 Sam. xxiv. 1; 1 Kings xxii. 20, 22.
[4] 1 Sam. vi. 19; 2 Sam. vi. 6 f.
[5] Isa. i. 11 ff.
[6] 2 Sam. xiii. 12.

the nobler aspirations of the human spirit; new vision must be contented with a few who have insight; it is a seed sown in hope, and builds on this, that time is on the side of truth, though time is slow; it reckons on this, that those who understand it are to be judged by value, not by number. So in this case too. The undercurrent of *higher spiritual life* was there since the days of the earliest post-Mosaic period, and it did not abate but rather deepened and spread, until in great and widely influential forms it attained the spiritual leadership and became a part of world-history.

Already in the early period of the Judges there appeared at the head of affairs in Debora, the God-inspired seer, one whose achievement it was not only to make a political unity of the tribes but to gather them about the banner of the God of Sinai. Thereby the thought of Yahweh as one of the baals of the land was consciously rejected. Israel's victory appeared to her as a vindication of Yahweh, and the comment that they ascribed their previous misfortunes to their falling away from Yahweh to " new gods ", the baals, sounds by no means incredible.[1]

The sacred ark in Shiloh, whatever it may have contained formerly, appears, since the time when Yahweh was enthroned upon the cherubs, to have been a centre of the imageless worship of Yahweh. Therefore, although its priests had much traffic with ephod and the teraphim, and it also becomes the object of timid superstition, yet the ark remained a weighty guardian of the precious tradition of the Mosaic period. Its Levite priests dating from the period of the wanderings[2] became, it is true, debased for a while, but at all times they firmly maintained

[1] Judges v. 11, 8.

[2] 1 Sam. ii. 27.

this element of the ancient inheritance; and after a short interval they restored that other element, namely, that to the ark from of old belonged a tent.[1]

THE DESERT-TENT.

There was another tent of equal, perhaps even greater, importance than this. In David's time there stood in or near Jerusalem, beside the tent in which the ark was kept, a second containing a shrine for the sacred oil horn and an altar in its inmost part.[2] There was no room for an altar beside the ark; if there was one belonging to the ark, its place was outside. This Yahweh-tent was therefore not that belonging to the ark, but an independent one.

It may be remembered that in the Mosaic history mention is in fact made of a desert-tent which had nothing to do with the ark and its tent which was strictly the place of revelation for Moses. Even though its relation to the ark remains obscure, there is no doubt of its existence.[3] We know well, however, that the southern tribes who, under the leadership of Judah, had taken possession of the Judean mountains and the neighbouring pasture lands, long maintained their nomadic habits of life.[4] Little wonder therefore that this ancient desert-tent which goes back to Moses' time had its place in Judah and its important devotees. Perhaps it had remained untouched at the conquest of Judah. At any rate it must have provided a strong inducement to the

[1] 2 Sam. vii. 6.

[2] 1 Kings ii. 28 ff., esp. 30 (come outside); cf. i. 39.

[3] Which tent is referred to in Joshua xviii. 1 is not clear—perhaps not even to the narrator.

[4] Especially the Kenites with Caleb or Jerahme'el; vide *Gesch.*, II^{3}, pp. 75, 188 (II^{6,7}, pp. 17, 106).

southern tribes that remained nomadic, and especially to Judah, to remain faithful to the Yahweh of Moses. Further, Baal had much less to offer to them than to their kinsmen of Ephraim. But with the rejection of Baal they were at the same time much further removed from all those perils which were involved in his worship. We have no reason to assume that the worship of Yahweh was here maintained in especially spiritual forms. The ancient Mosaic magical rites must at least have been further developed. But if only the exclusive and imageless worship of Yahweh was prized as Moses' bequest, Judah was thereby assured of a quite considerable advantage. It will also be scarcely an accident that it was precisely from Judah that Levites issued.[1] Still less was it an accident that Judah was at all times more religious than was Ephraim. Its faster adherence to the Mosaic tradition was its best protection.

Samuel.

Saul's personal religious position will have been very similar to the popular religion. On account of superstitious dread he renounced the ark which had been taken into captivity and merely retained the ephod. He paid homage to all kinds of superstition and savage practices.[2] For this reason his opponent Samuel took all the more trouble to maintain the purity of the Yahweh religion. His alienation from Saul was certainly due to a religious difference. The seer must have been grievously hurt at Saul's permanent neglect of the ark in the service of which Samuel had grown up. Also there is no

[1] Judges xvii. 7, xix. 1. The woman from Bethlehem leads us to expect Judah to be the home of the man.

[2] 1 Sam. xiv. 43 ff., xxviii. 3 ff.

decisive reason for refusing to ascribe to him the saying[1]:

> Obedience is more than finest offering
> And hearkening more than the fat of rams;
> For rebellion is a sin like divination,
> And evil desire is teraphim-sin!

It must be remembered that Saul in fact had repeatedly to do with diviners,[2] and further that his daughter kept a teraphim in the house.[3] But if the saying belongs to Samuel, it is perfectly clear that the assertion that in a difficult time he looked alone to a revival and purging of the debased religion for the salvation of his country,[4] is not merely the result of certain formal reflections. If in reality he ordered the suppression of sorcerers and stood with the old Mosaic forthrightness for the exclusive claims of Yahweh against every foreign god,[5] he certainly exalted the latter from the very beginning to be the fundamental principle of his political faith.

DAVID.

By subsequent ages David was reputed to have been not only the archetype of the ruler and extender of the kingdom, but also of the religious man. His name became the watchword for religious hope. It would be strange if the ideas of posterity had no foundation in fact. In reality he had a double nature which vibrated between ambition, passion, despotic caprice, and great-heartedness, tender-heartedness and fidelity in friendship. Such also he was in religion.

[1] 1 Sam. xv. 22 f.

[2] 1 Sam. xxviii. 7. In spite of verse 9, it will not have been the first occasion.

[3] 1 Sam. xix. 13 ff.

[4] 1 Sam. vii. 3 ff.

[5] 1 Sam. xxviii. 7 (certainly at Samuel's instigation), xv. 32 f.

He paid homage to the popular religion with full measure shaken down. He danced before the ark as was customary at the baal-festivals.[1] He harboured a teraphim in his house.[2] He allowed the descendants of Saul to be killed in Gibeon because of a savage superstition.[3] But he never forgot that he was the rival and successor of the man whose fate was brought about through disobedience to Samuel's teaching. It was this which made him restore the ark to honour and replace it in its ancient tent.[4]

He harboured in Jerusalem the ancient Judaic desert-tent of Yahweh[5]; he renounced the ephod; he abandoned the idea of building a magnificent temple[6] and deplored deeply his above-mentioned forced service of other gods.[7] In addition to all this he perseveringly advanced the process of the forcible suppression of Canaanite influences in Israel which others had begun. His whole behaviour indicated a leaning towards Moses and Israel's former desert life. We understand how David soon came to be regarded as the religious hero of his nation. It was through him that Jerusalem became at once the king's residence and the residence of God. Yahweh, Jerusalem and David's dynasty belong together.[8] More and more the forms of David and Zion grew to religious significance,[9] and if in the subsequent history of Israel one seeks an expression for their deepest longing for God's gracious help, it is only to be found in the expectation of an exalted son of David or a new David.[10] Whatever David's position may have been

[1] 2 Sam. vi. 14.
[2] 1 Sam. xix. 13.
[3] 2 Sam. xxi. 1 ff.
[4] 2 Sam. vi. 17.
[5] See above note, p. 81.
[6] 2 Sam. vii.
[7] 1 Sam. xxvi. 19.
[8] 2 Sam. vii.
[9] Cf. esp. Isa. x. 32–34, xiv. 32, xxix. 5–8, xxxi. 8 f.
[10] Isa. xi. 1 ff.; Mic. v. 1 ff. *et passim*.

in matters of detail, this lot would not have befallen a worshipper or devotee of Baal.

SOLOMON.

Solomon's figure does not stand out without blemish either in the judgment of his contemporaries or in that of later generations. He is reproached with having compromised with his foreign wives in the sphere of religion.[1] Many people must have reckoned his magnificent temple to Yahweh as a falling away from ancient Judaic custom and as a breach with the Mosaic tradition. The ancient tent was thereby discarded. This in fact involved a breach with the principles enunciated by Nathan and a concession to modern ideas. To these Solomon was open in other ways also, especially in culture and trade.[2] A retrograde movement in favour of Baal was feared, but on the whole the fear was disappointed. It may be left a moot point whether this was due to Solomon or to the conditions subsequent upon his death. Repeatedly in the following age the temple did not escape the danger of heathen influences. But the essential point is that Solomon took over the ancient ark of Moses unaltered from David's tent and therewith the traditions connected with it. The foremost of these was that no image of God was permitted in the temple beside the ark. The brazen serpent, which probably never entered into the temple itself, was not such an image.[3] It was simply a relic in the form of an attribute of God held sacred. Moreover the disappearance from Judah of proper names compounded with baal is significant and cuts away the ground from the constantly revived hypothesis that

[1] Kings xi. 1 ff. [2] See *Gesch.*, II[3], pp. 251 f. (II[6, 7], pp. 153 f.).
[3] See supra, p. 76.

Solomon was half or entirely a baal-worshipper. The rest was the result of the opposition with the north which set in shortly after Solomon's death; for the north after the time of Jeroboam I gave itself more and more consciously to the worship of Yahweh under the image of a bull. From this point of view it remains in fact, if not intentionally, an unquestioned achievement of Solomon that following in his father's footsteps he made the capital of Judah the permanent and unalterable home of that conception of Yahweh which in the course of events in Israel was led ever more strongly to assert itself in its traditional form against the encroachments of Canaanite worship in the north. Therefore, whatever his personal views may have been, Solomon, objectively viewed, was much more strongly on the side of the ancient Yahweh than of the new Yahweh-Baal.

The Earliest Prophets.

Meanwhile even before this time there had appeared upon the scene men, from outside the ruling classes, who spoke out powerfully for keeping the Yahweh-religion unstained. Their number increased with the progress of time. This was not the case in Judah alone but also in Ephraim. Just as Samuel once stood beside Saul as the embodiment of the king's conscience, so the prophets Nathan and Ahijah stood beside David and Solomon. Their names head the roll of those powerful figures who dared as free men to place themselves in the way of the authorities for warning or rebuke. They were worthy successors of Samuel with his "obedience is better than sacrifice", and their lodestar was nothing else than the struggle to prevent the Canaanite nature-worship from getting the upperhand in Israel and therewith on behalf of the ethical interpretation of Yahweh. The nation must not be allowed to lose the pattern which Moses had drawn. Words and thoughts such as those hurled at the king by Nathan in his famous "thou art the man" must have contributed more forcibly than anything else to revive the spirit of the old Mosaic Yahweh-laws and to overthrow the half popular conception of a God capricious and ethically indifferent.[1]

Writers Akin to Them.

If we know men such as Nathan and Ahijah by name, we may be sure there were others of their spirit whose names are lost to us, but who have left the mark of their spirit in their work. Even among those who present us with the history of the Judges we find a man who, in the story of Abimelech and his ignominious downfall, is evidently striving to illustrate the rule of Yahweh in ethical righteousness.[2] This was still more obviously the purpose of the narrator of David's family history, a man who belonged likewise to our period or more exactly to that of David's contemporaries.[3] In him we behold not only a narrator of the first rank, but, what is more, a man who tells the whole truth with indomitable courage. He does not shrink from revealing the blackest stains on the picture of the king whom he venerated. It is as if there lived in him something of the spirit of moral intensity and integrity which he ascribed to Yahweh as he knew him. In a few words he shows us step by step how David's guilt was visited upon himself and his house. His description is a vivid sermon: God

[1] See, further, pp. 129 f., on the historical situation see *Gesch.*, II3, p. 224 (II6, 7, pp. 133 f.).

[2] Judges, ix. esp. verses 56 f.

[3] 2 Sam. xiii–xx; cf. *Gesch.*, II3, pp. 290 f. (II6, 7, pp. 184 f.).

will not be mocked; history is the rule of a righteous God! Such thoughts as these must have been widely influential and must powerfully have affected the notion of the God ethically indifferent or placable by sacrifice. So at least some individuals there always were who outgrew the popular religion, and this spiritual upper class, a minority, constituted a leaven in the nation.

Yahwist and Elohist.

With the advance of time these movements attain more tangible form. Ever wider circles were led to outgrow the religion of the masses and therewith to a direct or indirect struggle against it. In the centre of the former stand Elijah and his followers, the leaders of the prophetic movement and the congregation they gathered about them. We must speak of them in their proper place. In the centre of the latter stand such men as the Yahwist and Elohist of the Pentateuch, the narrators of the primeval history whom, as their personal names are unknown to us, we have grown accustomed to call by their special names.

This is not the place in which to discuss them as narrators or as a literary school.[1] It will be enough to remind the reader that they were not only collectors of materials gained orally or through writing, but also great artists to whom it was given powerfully and faithfully to preserve with its own peculiarities that which came down to them. It was to be passed on to posterity worked over in a pleasing and artistic way, yet so as not to forfeit the peculiar fascination of originality fresh as the dew. In particular the Yahwist was himself far too much of a poet and artist

[1] Cf. *Gesch.*, II3, pp. 442 ff. (II6, 7, pp. 289 ff.).

not to prefer the inclusion of many narratives whose religious and ethical point of view had long since ceased to correspond with his own, rather than to intervene with a heavy hand and rub off the bloom of natural freshness.[1]

For men such as these Yahweh was in fact the only God. He was Lord of the whole world and Creator of heaven and earth, even though we do not find the express formulation of his uniqueness. Similarly all those strongly anthropomorphic representations of Yahweh, how he walked in the garden, came down from heaven, appeared bound to particular places and much more to the like effect,[2] are quietly reinterpreted into the form that this same God can do whatever he will, sees and finds his worshippers wherever he will, Israel in Egypt, Jacob and Elijah in the far east country.[3] Thus the narrator shows what Yahweh was and meant to himself, and that he himself was far beyond the limitations of the popular religion. The same is true of morality. One example will suffice. Though here and there Yahweh may be represented as ethically indifferent, yet in the story of the Fall (not as this may have been constructed in its most primitive and earliest form,[4] but as in the main we read it to-day) the God who punishes the wilful transgression of his command is no Being unconcerned with ethics, no mere power of Fate. For what we read to-day in Genesis iii. is no primitive tale but a representation based upon the fact of conscience and upon the command as the means for the securing of morality ; it is a story of the Fall properly so called dealing ethically with the problem of the origin of

[1] Cf. *Gesch.*, II³, p. 447 (II⁶, ⁷, p. 293).

[2] On these, see supra, pp. 79.

[3] Exod. i. ff. ; Gen. xxiv. 12 ff., xxix. 35, xxx. 30, xxxi. 11 f.

[4] On this, see *Gesch.*, I³, p. 371 (I⁵, ⁶, p. 220).

good and evil. Nothing shows more clearly how far exalted this God is above the ethically indifferent God of the popular religion than that Joseph himself can meet the heathen woman in Egypt with the saying: how could I do so great evil and sin against God?[1]

Sin was once again as with Moses a religious matter and God an ethical concept. This paved the way for the great prophets.

[1] Gen. xxxix. 9; see *Gesch.*, II³, pp. 446 f. (II⁶, ⁷, p. 293), and infra, pp. 96 f.

CHAPTER IV

THE FAITH AND THOUGHT OF ANCIENT ISRAEL

A SKETCH of the religion of Israel cannot omit thought-forms as they concern religion. With the advent of the classical prophets religion becomes to such an extent the central point of the national life that the inner history of the people in many respects coalesces with an exposition of that world of ideas in which these prophetic leaders and their followers moved. For the period of ancient Israel up to the point where the prophets laid the foundations for a new Israel, the idea of God and the ideas immediately connected therewith (the essential elements in the thought of any religion) may be deduced from the foregoing exposition. Certain further fundamental points follow herewith.

1. THE TRIBE AND THE FAMILY AS THE RELIGIOUS COMMUNITY.

Tribe and Family.—In ancient Israel the pillars of the religious life were the tribe and the family. The social life of nomad tribes was built up entirely upon the basis of natural blood-relationship. The family widened out into the kin and the tribe. The appointed priest for the family was the head of the house, for the kindred and tribe the eldest of the kin.[1] Accordingly natural blood-relationship in the

[1] Judges xvii. 5; Exod. xxiv. 5.

family and tribe constituted the most ancient religious community. Its most characteristic outward expression was common participation in the sacred rites. The Deity was called "the God of the fathers".[1] He was intimately bound up with the blood-kinship. In many cases a revelation to the tribal father or mother probably exercised a decisive influence. We call attention to the stories which the patriarchal sagas have to tell of Abraham and Jacob. Yahweh appeared to Abraham in Shechem; there he built him an altar. Jacob in his dream at Bethel felt the presence of God, and vowed to build a sanctuary on that spot.[2] Indeed, in that dim antiquity otherwise beyond the reach of recollection the connexion of the deity with the kinship must have been so close, that the god himself was claimed as a *blood-relation*. Only thus can we explain the proper names in which the deity is designated as father, brother or uncle: Abram, "father is the exalted One"; Aḥitub, "my (divine) brother is excellency"; Ammiel, "my uncle is god". Nathan's oracle to king David and his house affords us an excellent example of the manner in which in the process of time this relationship of physical-kinship was sublimated into one of moral obligation and mutual trust.[3] Thus the term "father", when it occurs as part of a proper name, will have acquired the significance of provider and counsellor, "brother" and "uncle" of protector.

Tribal Sacrifice.—Inasmuch as the ancient congregational cultus was essentially based on kinship, it is only natural that *sacrifice* was performed within the tribal circle. The story of David's hasty journey from

[1] Gen. xxviii. 13; Exod. iii. 6, 13 ff.

[2] Gen. xii. 6 f., xxviii. 13 ff., 22.

[3] 2 Sam. vii. 14: "I will be his father and he shall be my son."

Saul's court to his native Bethlehem, to celebrate there a tribal sacrifice on a particular day in the company of his fellow-tribesmen, is certainly only the continuation of the ancient custom.[1] The same is true of the sacrifice in fulfilment of a vow for which Absalom repaired from Jerusalem to Hebron and to which he invited two hundred guests for the accompanying feast.[2] Although Jerusalem was the resting-place of the ark and the royal cultus, Absalom went to his own birthplace,[3] which was also the capital of the whole tribe. Here dating from the days of David's sojourn in Hebron there apparently still stood a sanctuary of his immediate family circle ; here long after the establishment of the royal sanctuary in Jerusalem, the family festivals and festivals of members of the family were still held, while the festivals of the wider tribe were held in Bethlehem. Of course the sanctuary of the tribal king stood in some sort of relationship to that of the tribe itself. Hebron was from remotest ages a sacred place, which to this day has its oak of Abraham.

Further, in the ritual of the *Passover*, as it is described in Exodus xii., we see continuing into later days a trace of the family-sacrifice in which the head of the house played precisely the part of priest of the house. In these family and tribal sacrifices we are to observe the character of the sacrifice as pre-eminently a festival of fellowship expressed in a common meal.[4] The god being a blood-relation participated in the meal and fellowship as the pre-eminent member of the community. Moreover this explains also the significance of the ancient blood-rites. In the Passover the blood

[1] 1 Sam. xx. 6, 29. [2] 2 Sam. xv. 7, 11 f. [3] 2 Sam. ii. 8.

[4] The sacrifice was the deity's food, Lev. xxi. 8, 17. Those who were "invited" were the guests bidden by *Deity*, the pious man was the god's guest, *ger* ; cf. Ps. xv. and frequently elsewhere.

of the victim was sprinkled on the doorposts of the house; in earlier days it will doubtless have been on the entrance to the tent; in the case of other bloody sacrifices the blood was sprinkled on the altar or, in the case of especially important community festivals, half on the altar, the seat of the god, and the rest on the worshippers.[1] Man's portion was the flesh, the god's the blood; hereby the *kinship* of the god and his worshippers was re-established afresh, the seal was once again set to the blood-relationship

Village and District.—By Israel's entry into Canaan and into its settled life there the ancient tribal organization and with it the ancient tribal fellowship in the sacred services were jeopardized. The desert wanderer becomes homeless; kindred and tribe were home to him. The town and village dweller has his house and his own plot; his life is associated with the soil, and the soil becomes a home to him. We have already seen that field, tree and spring were the seat of the deity in Canaan. That was something which Israel also could not escape; its religion too had to attain a home-feeling in Canaan, and become indigenous to its soil. Henceforward the cultus was connected with field, village and locality, no longer with the family and the tribe. This at least was true in principle, that more and more the old order was replaced by the new.

Solomon, as is well known, gave the land a new constitution by dividing it into administrative districts, which in spite of the accommodation to the old order involved in fact a complete breach with the ancient tribal and kindred community organization.[2]

[1] Exod. xxiv. 6 ff. We should observe that blood-revenge was also a matter of blood-kinship, 2 Sam. xiv. 5 ff.

[2] See *Gesch.*, II^{3}, pp. 246 f., 272 (II^{6,7}, pp. 150, 176).

Even before this the ancient bonds of kinship had been greatly weakened by the *territorial* bond consisting of districts and localities. The people now came to sacrifice at the sanctuary nearest to their home and on festal occasions at the sanctuary of their district. So it was that Samuel's father with his family went on a pilgrimage to Shiloh for the annual festival.[1] So, too, Samuel conducts on the high place of the township where he lived a more important sacrificial feast to which he invited Saul and his servant.[2] Now, too, the priesthood of the head of the house or of the tribe was in process of dissolution. At fixed local sanctuaries, and more particularly at prominent cult centres, such as Shiloh, Dan and Jerusalem, certain priestly families were soon to be found; gradually they preferred descendants of Moses or of Levi. It stands to reason that even so the family as the social unit could not be altogether eliminated from the cultus. Not only could not the Passover be detached from it in spite of Deuteronomy's attempt to draw it more to Jerusalem,[3] but also, as we see in the case of Elkanah and all other pilgrims to a festival in every period, the members of the household accompanied the father to the festival as a matter of course, even though the rule prescribed the appearance only of males.[4] The consciousness of family-fellowship and of its near relation to God remained even in cases where the sense of tribal fellowship had begun to disappear. It is the case, as we should antecedently expect, that this process took place only by gradual stages, and that for a long time the sense of the fellowship of the kindred affected religious thought and practice alongside of

[1] 1 Sam. i. 21, ii. 19.
[2] 1 Sam. ix. 19 ff.
[3] Deut. xvi. 1 ff.
[4] Exod. xxxiv. 23.

territorial and local fellowship. Just as in the political sphere Saul found his mainstay in his own tribe, Benjamin, and David in Judah, so David journeyed to Bethlehem for the tribal sacrifice and Absalom to Hebron to fulfil a vow.[1]

2. Law and Religion.

Divine Law.—Tradition ascribes to Moses the character of being the source of Israelite law as well as that of founder of the religion. Yahweh was a pronounced God of law and morals, not only the originator and protector of both. So it comes about that from the time of Moses the peculiarity of Israel as contrasted with other peoples is that in Israel religion and ethics were far more closely associated than elsewhere. Hammurabi and other lawgivers of the ancient world know the combination, but in actual practice this tended to mean no more than that the god provided the stimulus to the legislation and confirmed its authority by means of a divine revelation. But in Israel we find even in the very oldest statutes, most expressly in the so-called Book of the Covenant, that the requirements of justice and the demands of religion, *jus* and *fas*, are treated absolutely as equivalents: the law of the altar is immediately followed by the law relating to slaves; the condemnation of magic and idolatry stands between sections dealing with obligations to the family and to strangers respectively; and these two statutes are themselves separated by the prohibition of unnatural sexual intercourse[2]; to blaspheme God and to curse the king are named in a single breath.[3] Accordingly Yahweh, though the conception of him is not

[1] Supra, p. 93.

[2] Exod. xx. 24 f. xxii., 15 ff.

[3] Exod. xxii. 27.

altogether free from ethical limitations, stood for law and morality in quite a different way from other gods. Joseph stigmatized adultery as sin against God; the murder committed by David and the judicial murder committed by Ahab were denounced by the prophets in the name of Yahweh and as injury done to his deity. It is then entirely in accord with the spirit of the ancient law when the so-called Law of Holiness includes every species of ordinance under the general sanction: for I am Yahweh, your God.[1] Precisely the same might be said of the regulations in the Book of the Covenant, for it is characteristic of the spirit of the ordinances of ancient Israel, which were fundamentally divine law.

Jurisdiction of the Priests and of the Laity.—In spite of all this, however, the separation between the two spheres of the sacred and the secular could not be altogether eliminated. This was in practice to a large extent unavoidable. Even in the early days the story is that Moses was constrained to groan under the pressing burden of those who resorted to him for justice. His father-in-law, Jethro, on the occasion of his visit found he must devise some means to relieve Moses, and he gave him the advice to divide the functions of justice: "choose for thyself from the people capable, god-fearing, trustworthy men who will not be bribed, and set them as prefects over 1,000, over 100, over 50 and 10, that they may be able at any time to deliver sentence for the people. It will then be necessary to bring before thee only the most important matters; the rest they can themselves decide." Moses, the man of God, retained the general oversight and the right of final decision, but little everyday affairs of justice were decided by the lay judiciary.[2]

[1] E.g. Lev. xx. 26, xxiv. 22, xxv. 55.

[2] Exod. xviii. 21 ff.

This clearly indicates a distinction between priestly and lay courts, between the sacred and secular judiciary, which was certainly important in post-Mosaic Israel, but probably obtained also even in the days of the wanderings ; for everywhere under nomadic conditions the head of the tribe, the sheik, is the natural magistrate, even though without executive power. In the course of time the place of these heads of the tribe was taken by the elders of the village or town, that is, by men of standing.[1] Their authority also was essentially a moral one ; but the closer organization of life in villages and towns naturally made the execution of their verdict much more sure than in the uncharted wilderness. The transitional period is represented by the so-called *Judges* (in the narrower sense), leaders of their tribe and neighbourhood, who certainly did not bear their title in vain.

Corresponding to the upbuilding and consolidation of a strong rule in the hand of the *king* we naturally find alongside of those local elders the royal governors and officials as secular judges with the king himself at their head as supreme magistrate.[2] It was in this capacity of judge that Absalom first appears.[3] The place of justice was the open space before the gate of the town, also the passage-way itself " in the gate " ; from Solomon's time there was also in Jerusalem the hall of justice which he built near the palace and temple.[4]

No proof is necessary that in addition to those mentioned above at every period judgment was given in the name of *God* by the priests and men of God

[1] 1 Kings xxi. 8 ff.

[2] Good illustrations of this are: 2 Sam. xiv. 4 ff., and 1 Kings iii. 16 ff.

[3] 2 Sam. xv. 2 ff.

[4] 1 Kings vii. 7.

or women of God like Debora, of whom it is expressly stated that she delivered judgment under a sacred tree.[1] Least of all is this remarkable in Israel in view of the mutual relationship which obtained there between the Deity and justice. None the less it is an interesting question, how the mutual relationship of the two departments was adjusted and conceived, and in what way the religious element made itself felt.

The Relation of the Two. The Divine Judgment and the Oath.—On the whole sacred justice was in the hands of the *priests*. Samuel, too, when he administered justice, may be looked upon as a priest.[2] None the less, as is exemplified by Debora, justice was sought for on occasion from inspired persons in general. Yet this would certainly be the case in secular ,everyday affairs rather than in matters deemed to belong to the sphere of sacred law. Should the citizen desire to know what became him in matters touching Yahweh and the ritual, especially in the distinction between clean and unclean, or what fine was required of him for an offence against the regulations of the temple or of the sacrifices, or what penance he must undergo to acquire again his forfeited religious status and all other problems of this kind, then it was to the priest that he repaired. The priest's sentence was the Torah, the divine prescription, the law, whether it were based upon a written or an unwritten code. The Torah was always sacred law. But the influence of religion was perceptible also in the secular sphere which was under the jurisdiction of the judges in distinction from the priests. If a case proved beyond the competence of the secular court, the decision was brought before God.[3] This *divine judgment* then converted a

[1] Judges iv. 4. [2] 1 Sam. vii. 16. [3] Exod. xxii. 7 f.

case of secular jurisdiction into a case of sacred. In that contingency the case came before the sanctuary and its priests.[1] A man was guilty, if God declared him so. In many cases the priest would consult the oracle, particularly the sacred lot, urim and thummim, and accommodate his sentence to its decision. So it was in the case of Achan's theft, so, too, in regard to the oversight of Jonathan who unwittingly had fallen under his father's curse.[2] The *oath* played a similar rôle. If a man were suspected of a crime, where witnesses were lacking, the suspect must clear himself of the suspicion by the " oath before Yahweh ".[3] That also involved the transference of a secular case to the sanctuary and the priests. Finally, this occurred in a particularly significant manner in cases of the so-called *divine ordeal.* In this instance, too, the case was straight away handed over to God ; but here, in distinction from the procedure indicated above as divine judgment, the decision was reached not through the mediation of the priest in the sacred lot or oracle, but immediately through divine intervention. Curses written upon a sheet were put in water which was harmless to the innocent but poison to the guilty.[4]

The Prophets.—If religion distinctly took control of certain legal cases which of themselves pertained to the secular judges, there is nothing here which distinguishes Israel from other peoples. Above all the oath and the ordeal are widespread. All the more remarkable is the peculiar relationship between the legal and the religious which we find in the case of the *prophets.* What Moses had incited was here

[1] Deut. xix. 17.

[2] Joshua vii. 16 ff. ; 1 Sam. xiv. 40 ff.

[3] Exod. xxii. 9 f. ; Lev. v. 22 ; 1 Kings viii. 31.

[4] Num. v. 11 ff

brought to perfection. We may call ideal the way in which honest dealings and impartial justice were claimed as pertaining to the chief requirements of Yahweh and the religion of Israel. By contrast with this we feel all the more strongly the lapse from this height when the post-prophetic development forced the religious life into the bonds of external laws concerning themselves little about the spirit which had inspired the prophets.

3. Death and the Beyond.

Ideas Connected with Interments.—Its ideas of death and of what lies beyond form an important standard by which the peculiarity and developments of every religion may be measured. Men's ideas of the fate of the dead may be deduced from the manner of their funeral customs. The greatest importance was attached to the actual interment; to lack burial counted as the greatest deprivation; this fate was decreed fitting only for the condemned and those under a curse.[1] Saul's faithful servants stole the king's body, his concubine Rizpah protected her sons' bodies day and night that they might have burial.[2] This is only intelligible if burial was not merely a custom, but also a sacred duty and a right pertaining to every man. Lack of burial brought severe injury to the deceased; the soul's peace was jeopardized; it was constrained to *roam* restlessly about. Such souls could be heard mournfully whimpering and wailing in remote spots.[3] For the soul clave to the body and its fate was closely bound up with the fate of the body. Such was Antigone's point of view;

[1] 2 Kings ix. 10; Jer. xxv. 33.
[2] 1 Sam. xxxi. 11 ff.; 2 Sam. xxi. 10.
[3] Isa. xxix. 4; cf. viii. 19. An exception, Jer. xxxi. 15.

she recked therefore of no prohibition where family duty was concerned. We may compare also the Phœnician king Eshmunazar who on his sarcophagus makes the urgent appeal not to disturb his peace and invokes a curse on anyone who should scatter his bones.[1] If any man would pursue an enemy even after death and dishonour his memory, he would destroy his dead body or leave it for animals to consume.[2]

Precautionary Measures. Homage.—Even this proves that in Israel death was not supposed to mark the end of all existence and life whatsoever. The dead lived on, only in another mode and another form, and due care must be taken that he do not bring *misfortune* upon the living. The Canaanites effected this by means of offerings of food, drink and all manner of gifts.[3] Not otherwise will it have been in Israel. In addition, it was effected by various precautionary measures; men muffled up their hair and beard to protect themselves from the influence of the dead; they scattered earth on their heads to make themselves unrecognizable to the dead.[4] They went further: one durst not have for an enemy so fearsome a being as a dead man's spirit; for it belonged to the ranks of *higher existences*, mysterious, powerful spirits, described by the general term *elohim*[5]; as such it possessed superhuman knowledge and power. Such beings were invoked for information.[6] Men gashed

[1] Lidzbarski, *Handb. d. Nordsem. Epigraphik* I., p. 141.

[2] Amos ii. 1; 2 Kings ix. 10; Jer. xxv. 33; cf. 1 Sam. xxxi. 9 f.; 2 Sam. xxi. 10.

[3] See *Gesch.*, I5,6, in the index under the heading "Totenbestattung".

[4] 2 Sam. xv. 30, iv. 12.

[5] 1 Sam. xxviii. 13.

[6] 1 Sam. xxviii. 7 ff; Isa. viii. 19; Deut. xviii. 11.

themselves till the blood flowed, just as was done at the Baal altar to the Baal, to gain the attention of the dead or to mollify them.[1] The dead were also feasted with meals in their honour like the celebrations in honour of the tribal deities, that is to say, the ancestors. Men cropped their hair and beard in precisely the same way as hair was offered to a god.[2] Men took off their shoes in the presence of the dead, went about naked or in sackcloth, precisely as they did in the presence of the Deity or had done in days gone by.[3] We should not be surprised therefore that reverence was paid to the dead quite as if they were divine beings. According to the narrative of E, Jacob erected in Bethel upon the grave of his mother's nurse under the oak of lamentation a tombstone which was anointed with oil and had water poured over it.[4] This has all the appearance of a *sacrifice* offered to the spirit of the departed.

The Origin of this Belief and its Overthrow.—Unhappily we have no knowledge how many of these ideas Israel brought with it out of the period of the wanderings and how many were adopted in Canaan; for we may assume with a high degree of probability that the Canaanites possessed in the main these same ideas and practices before Israel entered the country.[5] One is tempted therefore to characterize this whole circle of ideas simply as Canaanite; but against this we may accept it as a fact that in this connexion there was a far spread community of ideas amongst the peoples of the same grade of civilization stretching in part

1 Deut. xiv. 1; Lev. xxi. 5; cf. 1 Kings xviii. 21 f.

2 Deut. xxvi. 14; Jer. xvi. 7; cf. Dalman, *Petra*, p. 62; Lev. xxi. 5; cf. *Iliad*, xxiii. 135, 152 f.

3 Ezek. xxiv. 17; Isa. xxxii. 11; cf. Exod. iii. 5.

4 Gen. xxxv. 8; cf. verses 19 f.

5 See supra, p. 102, note 3.

even as far as Greece. It is a still weightier argument to the contrary that we know of a place where Israel sojourned in the wilderness which bears the name of Oboth, that is, spirits of the dead [1]; this must have been the scene of such a cult. These ideas then should be regarded as part of Israel's inheritance from past ages derived from both these two sources, namely, the influences of the period of the wanderings and of their association with the native Canaanites.

At another point also we are thrown back upon conjecture. There is no doubt that under the influence of the Yahweh religion there was a tendency from early times in Israel to challenge these ideas of the dead. The reverence and worship shown to the dead was inconsistent with the exclusive claims of Yahweh and imperilled them. The worship of the dead was declared forbidden and everything connected therewith was prohibited. The dead body itself and the house in which it lay were unclean.[2] According to a credible account Saul dismissed from the country those who resorted to necromancy.[3] But we know neither how far the prohibition of those customs and practices was carried through, nor how widespread among the people were those customs and their underlying ideas. We know that the prophets and probably many of the priests also energetically attacked them, very likely without abolishing them. Still, they created a group to combat these superstitions. Much that belongs to this subject comes to us only through the medium of linguistic usage or in poetry. Likewise we know that the prophetic movement and the prophetic point of view gradually

[1] Num. xxi. 10 f., xxxiii. 43 f.
[2] Num. xix. 11 ff.; Jer. xvi. 5 ff.
[3] 1 Sam. xxviii. 7.

advanced like the tide. Long before Amos' time there was a group of men who, on decisive points, agreed with him and his followers.

The Idea of Sheol.—What was the fate of the interred? They went to their fathers or fellow-tribesmen.[1] With them they dwelt together in the family grave which frequently was in their own house or palace.[2] Here under exceptional circumstances they might be observed; so it was that Rachel, the tribal mother, was heard bemoaning the ruin of the house of Joseph and Benjamin near her grave in Ramah.[3] That was only one of the conceptions, probably a more primitive one; even in early days, but increasingly as time went on, and possibly under the influence of the Babylonian conception of Hades as situated on a high mountain-top,[4] men formed the picture of a vast subterranean hollow space, a sort of universal grave, called Sheol. Here the dead lived a shadowy joyless existence; without memory and with senses dulled they were the victims of a melancholy dreamlike brooding.[5] Where the representation of the next world radically differs from this, as in the powerful poem Isaiah xiv., we are dealing with isolated poetical developments due in part to foreign influence.

On consideration these facts show beyond cavil that the whole circle of ideas connected with the continued life and activity of the dead was foreign to the religion of Yahweh. Apart from the Sheol idea every element is equally well or even better conceived as Canaanite or common property rather than exclusively

[1] Gen. xv. 15, xlvii. 30, xlix. 29, 33.

[2] 1 Sam. xxv. 1, xxviii. 3; 1 Kings ii. 34.

[3] Jer. xxxi. 15.

[4] Jastrow, *Bab. Rel.*, I., p. 157.

[5] Ps. vi. 8, xxx. 10; Job xiv. 21 f. Their name, Refa'im = flabby or powerless ones.

Hebrew. It is a fragment of that animistic viewpoint which the Yahweh religion was for a long time powerless to overcome. So deep had it sunk into the hearts of the people, so closely bound up was it with their most deeply rooted customs, that through all the centuries it maintained its tenacious hold.

Hopes of a Return to Life.—It should occasion no surprise that there is no place here either for the thought of any connexion between conditions yonder and the ethical life here or for the conception of a return. Yet neither notion could be permanently excluded. The former makes its first appearance only late, particularly in Enoch. The latter made itself felt much earlier, at least in vague forms and daring glimpses. At first, to be sure, the natural consequence of that point of view was absolute hopelessness. Job still complained: "as water flows out of the sea, so man lies down and wakes not again", and David said of his dead child, "he will not come to me, but I shall go to him".[1] But in a religion like that of Israel this could not remain permanently the case. Once prophecy had grasped the thought that Yahweh's love was mightier than Israel's sin, as we find in the teaching of Hosea and Jeremiah, once the pious reflection, especially of the psalmists, had grasped the value of fellowship with God and of life in him as alone worth living, further conclusions were bound to follow. These we find in passages like Ezekiel xxxvii. applied to the nation; but that meant that in principle at least the spell was broken; should that which was possible in the case of the people as a whole be ruled out for the individual? The question became more urgent with the increasing value placed upon the individual

[1] Job xiv. 12 ff., xxi. 26; 2 Sam. xii. 23.

life. It could not be left unanswered. Individual poets with the daring grasp of faith tore aside the veil at least for a moment,[1] until at last full assurance was won and clearly proclaimed.[2]

But all that is beyond the limits of ancient Israel. In those early days men appear to have been satisfied if their names were treasured in the thoughts of their posterity.[3]

4. Expectations of the Future.

Expectations Held in Common by the Nations.—In ancient Israel the less the individual's own expectations for the future, the keener were his hopes for the community as a whole. It must have been the case in Israel as in the rest of the ancient world that even in early days expectations and oracles were current concerning a coming age of blessing, a golden age, which should banish all fears of a threatening period of curse.[4] As the beginning of the world was pictured as an age of complete bliss and with the peace of Paradise, so also the end. The present sufferings should be banished, and Yahweh himself should be the inaugurator of this turning-point of the ages. This train of thought we can infer with a high degree of probability, though no positive proof of it can be

[1] Ps. xvii. 15, xlix. 16, lxxiii. 26; Job xix. 25 ff. How far the thought of a return to life after death advocated in the Adonis cult may have proved fruitful in influence is a problem which deserves further careful consideration. Cf. Sellin in *Neu. kirchl. Zeitschr.*, 30, pp. 232 ff.

[2] Isa. xxvi. 18 f., xxv. 8; Dan. xii. 2 f.; Enoch li.–liv., lxi. 5, etc. The first indication of a distinction in the fate of men is Ezek. xxxii. 17–32.

[3] 2 Sam. xviii. 18; 1 Sam. xv. 12.

[4] Apart from Amos v. 18, dealing with the Day of Yahweh, we find traces of this particularly in Isa. vii. 14 ff. [milk and honey correspond to nectar and ambrosia], and Isa. xi. 6 ff. [Paradise].

adduced.[1] Indeed, even the thought of a coming Helper who should inaugurate the expected time of blessing would seem to have already existed; for when the prophets first began to speak of the holy remnant which should survive the periods of distress or of God's Day, or when the poets for the first time spoke of the great Helper who should come, they assume that these ideas were already well known.[2] Hence they are never actually described, but merely referred to as familiar to everybody. Every blessing which the future was to vouchsafe was, as Amos teaches us, long before his time summed up in the thought of the Day of Yahweh.

Oracles in Israel.—Those universal expectations common to the nations would appear, in the case of Israel, to have been gathered up in *popular* compositions without ethical interest. One must suppose that most probably they were derived from and expanded by seers attached to powerful houses and, later on, to royal courts. We know not only that David had such men round about him, but also that attached to the court of Ahab were four hundred prophets whose oracle should proclaim the issue of his campaigns.[3] In this connexion we also know further that long before David actually attained the crown, he received all manner of oracles predicting his succession to Saul.[4] Only so do we get a satisfactory explanation of Saul's deadly hatred of him.

[1] Certain cosmological expectations of doom are earliest attested, the darkening of the sun and moon, the destruction of the world by fire, a great flood.

[2] Amos v. 15; Isa. vii. 3; Amos v. 18; Gen. xlix. 8 ff.; Num. xxiv. 17.

[3] 1 Kings xxii. 6 ff.

[4] Cf. 2 Sam. iii. 18, v. 2, and in that connexion *Gesch. d. V. Isr.*, II[3], p. 192, note 2, and p. 477, note 2.

In this way, too, we can account for a word in the oracles of Balaam which by virtue of its reference to Agag can only be dated as belonging to the time of Saul or the earlier years of David. Once David was king of Jerusalem, the comparison of his power with that of Agag was pointless. It fits best the time when David was being persecuted by Saul. A seer had observed a "star out of Jacob, a sceptre out of Israel" rising in the sky.[1] Of him he said, "I see him but not nigh, I behold him but not yet". These are significant figurative phrases of an intentionally mysterious secrecy, half revealing, half concealing. But the meaning of the oracle was sufficiently transparent, at any rate to those whom it concerned: there shall appear on Israel's throne a glorious ruler whose light should shine far and wide, and who should bring to a close the wars with the hostile neighbours in the south. The seer can refer only to David, but the manner in which he names him has a further significance; to him David is "he", the seer beholds in David the "him"—the long expected emissary of Yahweh. Ever and again to this day in celebrations of Allah the Dervishes cry out: "He! He!" But in our case not Yahweh is meant but his emissary.

David.—Another similar oracle belongs to David's earlier period. The so-called blessing of Jacob is a collection of oracles relating to the individual tribes, dating for the most part from the later part of the period of the Judges. Of Judah which had risen up like a young lion from the spoil and was about to assume the hegemony among the tribes through the instrumentality of David, it was said by a seer that the sceptre and the wand of office shall not be taken

[1] Num. xxiv. 17; Agag (from Amalek) in verse 7.

from him "till he comes whose right it is"[1]; that means, until the times of the greater king to whom an even greater dominion pertains. But the manner in which David is referred to and a glimpse beyond him is offered, is another illustration of the peculiar allusive style of the seers couched in the language of the thoughts and expectations that were so current on everybody's lips, that they needed but to be hinted at. Balaam's diction gives us the key to the interpretations of the Jacob oracle.

In David's heyday when he had attained to the height of his power, a seer attached to his court, Nathan, further developed those ideas.[2] He corroborated the statement that the sceptre should not be taken from Judah; the kingship should permanently remain with the house of David, "I will make thee an house". This saying also would be a purely external interpretation within the limits of national and dynastic aspirations. But when it is added of the future kings of the house of David that "he shall be to me a son, and I will be a Father to him. If he commit iniquity, I will chasten him with the rod of men", we observe that the expectation has passed over into other territory. The addition as well as the first clause make it clear that the sonship is conceived as a relationship of adoption upon an *ethical* basis.[3] Thus an expectation, which in itself was ethically indifferent and alongside of its national significance was rather allied with cosmological than with ethical ideas, was by these means translated to the ethical sphere.

The Yahwist.—It is precisely these elements which we find further developed in certain oracles preserved

[1] Gen. xlix. 8 ff.; cf. in this connexion *Gesch.*, II^3, p. 311 (II $^{6, 7}$, p. 204[1]).

[2] 2 Sam. vii. 14 ff. On the date *Gesch.*, II^3, p. 210 (II$^{6, 7}$, p. 123).

[3] Cf. Ps. ii. 7.

in the J narratives. The thought of a great future continued; but it is there prized in circles other than those connected with the persons of power. This gives us an inkling of the wide diffusion of the idea and at the same time of the diversity of its detailed presentation. The oracle which brings man's suffering into connexion with his fall and therein lays serpent, woman and man under a grievous curse, yet does not end upon the note of curse and suffering; the seed of the woman " shall bruise thy head, and thou shalt bruise his heel ".[1] In the present form of the story the serpent is the seducer, its seed the powers that tempt and entice to evil. Here we are on the ethical-religious plain. Man is appointed to battle; his whole life long he must strive against sin and temptation. But his victory in the end is certain. Through whom? and how? Yahweh may reveal that in the future. But the victory is assured, the serpent shall be destroyed. This postulates an expectation of the future, or, rather, we have here the reaffirmation of the ancient expectation delivered from the sphere of the national and dynastic into the realm of universal ethics.

The Messiah and the Day of God.—Under this heading various strands of development are obviously revealed. Men cherished the hope of a great and fortunate turn in affairs; in the forefront of the picture stood an unknown, but great and powerful deliverer. Correspondingly men looked for a powerful and enduring kingship in Judah derived from the stock of David. It was not expressly stated that this deliverer was to be the king of David's house. Finally dawned the hope of an ethical development culminating in the victory of the good. Each of these trains of

[1] Gen. iii. 15 f.

thought could be carried on independently; their confluence in the thought of the future son of David as the promised deliverer who should inaugurate a reign of peace and righteousness was the merit of *Isaiah* and of prophecy.[1] Thus the popular national expectation coalesced with the ethical-religious expectation, and together they formed the *Messianic idea.* And Amos by giving a completely new content to the long familiar notion of the Day of God as the day of judgment for Israel's sin, created an eschatology with an ethical motive as counterpart to an ethically conditioned Messianic idea.[2] Henceforward these two sets of ideas must march hand in hand. This, however, does not preclude the possibility of their continued existence and of separate development.[3]

5. Foreign Influences.

Panbabylonism.—For a long time the peculiarity of the religion of Israel was supposed to lie precisely in its seclusion from foreign influences. "The people, it dwells alone and shall not be reckoned among the nations"—this sentence[4] was for a long time thought to hold good of their religion also and of itself to guarantee its privileged uniqueness. When, therefore, pre-eminently through the astonishing discoveries in the field of oriental archæology, it came to be realized that in point of fact many paths cross and recross, and that the religion of Israel also is only intelligible by the method of the comparative study of religions, there was imminent danger of a reaction to the other extreme. If in earlier days Israel had been isolated in a one-sided way, now came the tendency with an even greater one-sidedness to let its peculiarity be

[1] Esp. Isa. ix. 1 ff., xi. 1 ff.

[2] Amos v. 18 ff.

[3] See further, p. 113.

[4] Num. xxiii. 9.

absolutely submerged in the stream of universal development. Israel was made to appear as a mere spiritual province of Egypt or even more of Babylon. It is a question of determining the influence and stimulus exercised on Israel by the outside world, but of avoiding Panbabylonism and Panorientalism.

The Messianic Idea. Mythical Motifs.—The field of expectations of the future which we considered above and in which we recognized certain common ideas as already existing in Canaan before the time of Israel, has in recent times been treated in such a way as if the whole scheme of Messianic prophecy had been simply taken over by Israel from without.[1] The figure of the redeemer, too, was supposed to have existed in Egypt and Babylon, and men spoke even of a non-Israelite " expectation of redemption " and of an Egyptian " Messianic king ". But nowhere in Babylon is to be found just the essential figure, namely, a future royal son of God who was to establish a reign of blessedness and peace. The salvation expected in Babylon was not conceived eschatologically as connected with the end of the days and as occurring at the turning-point of history, but as occurring in the present world-order. So, too, the Babylonian " son of God " was simply the reigning monarch. In the same way it is highly probable that there was no thought in Egypt of a redeemer king belonging to the last age, as was originally supposed, but merely of a definite historical king (Amenemhet I) and a definite historical disaster.[2]

[1] Eduard Meyer, *Die Israeliten*, etc., 1906, pp. 451 f.; Zimmern, *Die Keilinschriften u. d. A.T.*, 3, pp. 380 f.; Bertholet, art. " Eschatologie " in *Relig. in Gesch. u. Gegenw.*, II.; also the texts and comments in Gressmann's *Texte und Bilder zum A.T.*, 1909, I., pp. 204 ff.

[2] Cf. Kittel, *Alttestam. Wissensch.*, 3 ed. [1917], pp. 228 ff., 4 ed. [1920], p. 244.

Much the same applies to the school of Winckler with its tendency to mythologize, to allegorize and to discover beneath the obvious interpretation some deeper significance recognized by the initiate alone.[1] However certain it may be that in Babylon the wisdom and speculation of the priesthood played a conspicuous part, so little proof have we that within Israel and the Old Testament, more particularly prior to the Babylonian exile, any parallel movement of thought was widespread. Above all it will not do, especially when unvarnished facts of ordinary life are before us, to discover in them hidden references to Babylonian astral myths, nor to represent the natural speech of a simple peasant people as being replete with mystical " motifs " or intentional or unintentional allusions to Babylonian myths and astral symbols; this is to abandon the solid ground of sober-minded science for the dangerous but seductive realm of phantasy.

Babylon.—While it is necessary for us carefully to guard against exaggeration, yet with all the more discrimination we must stress the measure of foreign influences upon Israel's religion which can really be proven. There are three main fields to consider, Babylon, Egypt and Canaan.

With regard to Babylon we must bear in mind that at the very least since the time of Ḥammurabi, in fact ever since the midde of the third millennium, a strong political and cultural predominance of Babylonian influence made itself felt in Syria and Palestine. That cannot have left religion unaffected. Since 2000 B.C. we find Nergal and later Ninib also and Ashirat, closely connected with Ishtar, as deities

[1] Cf. particularly his *Geschichte Israels*, I, II. [in *Geschichte in Einzeldarstellungen*].

in Canaan. Under the prevailing political conditions the code of Ḥammurabi must early have reached Canaan. The constant and often intimate correspondence between this code and sections of the so-called Mosaic law justifies the inference that Israel in the post-Mosaic period came under the influence of this code.[1] The Amarna-texts and the clay tablets from Taanach prove to us further that the Babylonian script was written in Palestine shortly after the middle of the second millennium B.C. Babylonian texts therefore were also read, and among these doubtless some of religious import. In this connexion it is most natural to suppose that the close connexion between the Biblical narratives of the Creation and Flood and the Babylonian texts of the same content is due to the mediation of the Canaanites who had adopted those stories prior to the arrival of Israel. Much the same may be true of the psalmody, all the more because we have good reason to assume ancient Canaanite songs of this sort.[2]

Immediate Influence.—If all these contributory elements are to be considered as mediated through the inhabitants of the country, then since the time of Solomon and still more since the time of Omri, owing to the renewed political contact, the influences of Babylon may have come to Israel direct. Solomon's temple indicates not merely Syrian and Hittite, but also in a remarkable degree Assyrian influences, and his mercantile enterprises doubtless extended eastwards and afforded opportunity for all manner of Assyrian religious influences to stream in upon Israel. At any rate after the time of Omri and Ahab there was scarcely any intermission of that close contact

[1] In that connexion, see Kittel, *Altt. Wiss.*, ch. iv, section 2.
[2] See Kittel, *Gesch.*, I[3], p. 199 (I[5, 6], p. 160) (following Böhl).

often so unwelcome to Israel. Ahaz of Judah was also a religious vassal of Assyria, still more so was Manasseh.[1] Although in this late period the religious practice of Jerusalem in part at least sank to a mere imitation of what prevailed in Assyria, yet as regards the earlier period, more particularly in regard to the saga-material which comes to us through the Yahwist and the Elohist, so far as these betray Babylonian influence, we must emphasize and commend the remarkable independence with which they rejected or amended polytheistic ideas and such as were beneath Israel. We are dealing here not so much with a case of borrowing as of a rebirth due to the spirit of the Yahweh religion. Even where in Israelite poets, especially in the prophets and psalmists, references to Babylonian or other myths recur, they enjoy for the most part no independent life of their own, but are steeped in the thought-forms of Israel.[2] It is not before Ezekiel and Zechariah that we find a widespread adoption of Babylonian material little altered.

Egypt.—Canaan's connexion with Egypt is marked by the facts that since ancient times there was a brisk trade between the two countries, and that from the time of Thutmosis III Palestine actually became an Egyptian province. Egyptian garrisons and governors with their officials were to be found up and down the country. They naturally brought their Egyptian gods with them. Scarabs are found in numbers dating from as early as 2000 B.C. The seal of Atanaḫili represents Egyptian symbols as well as the Babylonian deity. Ashtart in the form of Hathor,

[1] See *Gesch.*, II³, pp. 534 f, 574 ff. (II⁶, ⁷, pp. 364, 393 ff.).

[2] This is especially true of ideas such as that of Tiāmat [tehōm], Rahab, the mountain of the gods in the north and the like.

Amon, Ptah and Bes were worshipped. Ramses III erected a temple of Amon in Syria, where the princes of the country deposited their tribute, and the temple of Amon in Thebes possessed as its property a number of towns in the country.[1] One can see how widespread was Egyptian religious influence in Palestine. That situation did not suddenly pass away when Israel entered the country, rather it offered to the new-comers from Egypt a further opportunity to take a stand against Egyptian religion. If by their flight from Egypt they had escaped one pressing danger, here they met with another. If in our sources we find less reference to the danger of the influences of the Egyptian religion than of those of the baal-worship, this should not blind us to the fact of the danger. Complaints like that of Isaiah[2] of the number of foreign gods in the land give us every warrant for thinking also of Egypt; and this too all the more because Solomon had a daughter of the Pharaoh among his wives, and in his reign the influence of Egypt was renewed. This was naturally increased with the revival of contacts with the Nile country after the time of Isaiah, and thereafter they were continuous.[3]

But we should do wrong if we spoke only of dangers pressing Israel from this quarter. In ancient days there flourished in Egypt a highly developed proverbial wisdom. In the same way Egypt enjoyed long before Israel religious lyrics in the form of hymns to the deity or of odes of thanksgiving. This was a source of valuable stimulus to Israel none the less significant in that as in the case of the Babylonian material so

[1] *Gesch.*, I[3], p. 556; II[3], p. 55 (I[5, 6], p. 363, II[6, 7], p. 1).
[2] Isa. ii. 8.
[3] Cf. particularly Isa. xxx. and xxxi.

here the religion of Israel preserved its complete independence.

Canaan. The Language of the Cultus.—Only the inhabitants of the land can have introduced Israel to the religious impressions which had been made upon Canaan in the pre-Mosaic period by Babylon and Egypt. Even in later times the same mediators doubtless played a highly important part. But the Canaanites also enjoyed a not unimportant civilization of their own, and we have seen in the preceding chapter how vividly it affected Israel. No more need here be said of the significance for Israel's religion of the Baal and Ashtart cults, nor of the sanctuaries indigenous to its soil and their festivals. It will suffice to mention several other points. The language of Israel was the language of Canaan; the word for God, *Elohim*, and all other religious concepts Israel shared with the inhabitants of the land. The same holds good of a number of local and personal names and particularly of the terminology connected with the cultus. We must beware of drawing too hasty conclusions from this. If 'Ain-semes, sun-spring, and 'Obed-edom, worshipper of Edom, point beyond doubt to a cult of the sun and to the worship of a god Edom, it does not by any means follow that both deities had been taken over by Israel from Canaan. The names might be taken over just as the early Christians chose the name Isidor without wishing for a moment to be taken for worshippers of Isis, and as a chieftain of the Mosaic period was named Hur after the Egyptian Horus. In just the same way if the sacrificial language referred to the sacrifice as God's food [1] and to the odour of the sacrifice as a "mollifying odour", the underlying ideas are clearly

[1] Lev. xxi. 6, 8, 17.

of an angry god to be pacified with a pleasant odour and of a hungry god to be satisfied with sacrifice; but, unless further evidence can be adduced, we have no right to infer that Israel associated these ideas with its Yahweh.

Canaan. Stories and Myths. Higher Ideas.—If we inquire what material Israel took over from the Canaanites, we shall be right to think in the first place of narratives closely connected with the soil, such as that of the destruction of Sodom and Gomorrah or of Jacob's struggle at Peniel with the river-god of Jabbok.[1] Ancient Canaan, as we should anticipate from the rest of its spiritual life, must have possessed rich material of stories of the gods. Beyond doubt much of this passed over to Israel and was fundamentally reconstructed in its transfer to Yahweh. Where this was successful, the original narrative can no longer be identified by us except perhaps in part. Where it was intractable, as in the myth of the marriage of the sons of God, Gen. vi., it can be all the more clearly recognized as borrowed. That the story comes down to us at all is due merely to the circumstance that the Yahwist concurs with the sentence of condemnation expressed in verse 3 against the profanation. Only this circumstance preserved the story. Other narratives, not sharing in this lot, are lost, and it is only from certain allusions that we can infer that once they were there and troubled Israel. Thus we can with some certainty divine from various indications that Israel also was cognizant of the Canaanite and Phœnician Adonis-myth which was closely connected with the myth of Osiris in Egypt and of Tammuz in Babylon, together with its expression of the mourning for the decay of the vegetation and

[1] Gen. xviii f., xxxii. 25 ff.

joy at the re-awakening of life. A similar source must be ascribed to the notion of Yahweh as a healing God, the physician of Israel. The two ideas are closely connected; the deity who bestows life was at the same time the deity who keeps alive, delivers from sickness and redeems from death. This seems also the origin of the notion of the deity as helper and redeemer.[1] In the same way it seems that we should ascribe to stimulus from Asia Minor and Thrace and still more from Canaan the thought of near personal relationship with the deity pointing to the indwelling of God in man and then on a higher plain to a close ethical fellowship with God. The former stimulated the surrender of self in mysticism and ecstasy, the latter the permanent indwelling of God in man. Such Phœnician proper names as Ohelbaal, Ohelmilk describe the worshipper as the tent, that is, the habitation of the deity.

Herein is found a trait which, it must be admitted, is alien to the real Yahweh religion. The God of Moses and of the prophets was an austere God, just and exalted and a consuming fire. When we find him represented by individual prophets and then later by the psalmists as a God of love and of fellowship, we see the fruits of the contact with Canaan. On the other hand, if the God of the Fathers in distinction from the God of Moses calls to mind the influence of Canaan, we have there perhaps yet another reason for refusing to regard that picture of him as the groundless delineation of later phantasy. But in any case we shall be wise to conclude that if the danger which threatened Israel from Canaan was great, Israel received from Canaan not only dangers but also much valuable stimulus in directions which would have been

[1] Baudissin, *Adonis u. Esmun*, pp. 511 ff.

remote from the natural bent of the Yahweh religion. And on the other side our impression of the superlative greatness of the religion of Moses is heightened, when we appreciate the vitality that was in it not only to reject foreign elements which it regarded as precarious but also to welcome other elements which were in the line of its own enrichment.

CHAPTER V

PROPHECY AND THE GREAT PROPHETS OF THE ASSYRIAN PERIOD

ITS SIGNIFICANCE.

The world over the emotions that drag man down into the abyss are stronger than those that exalt him. In the third chapter we have proved adequately how great was the danger which threatened the Hebrew religion from the side of the Canaanite baal religion. But for a timely reaction the Mosaic Yahweh-religion would certainly have succumbed to the fate of being swallowed up by that nature-religion which was so closely associated with the land and its inhabitants. This reaction was brought about by a movement, the initiators of which called themselves *nabi*, *nebi'im*, to whom we have long been accustomed to give the name of prophet. Israel had to thank them alone for having been led past the edge of the precipice, and for the fact that its religion, although only in a portion of the ancient nation, finally survived for the world and for history. The fate of Ephraim and of Judah gives striking proof of this. The exclusive cause why the ten tribes of the northern Israelite State, shortly after being transplanted to a foreign soil, sank into oblivion there, and all trace of them is ultimately lost to history, lies in the circumstance that they had long ceased to have any peculiar religious life which in a conspicuous way would have marked them off from the religions of the people among whom their lot was cast. For at the stage attained by peoples like Israel and by nations similarly placed, it is religion that binds them together and gives them their distinguishing characteristics. At a quite different stage of development the East to-day provides us with ample illustration of this. On the other hand, the reason why Judah was not completely absorbed by Babylon, but retained in part its characteristics and celebrated its return from exile, is again to be sought solely in the fact that in the meanwhile the preaching of the prophets had so far gained ground that it seemed impossible for Judah to go over to the Babylonian religion and be merged in the Babylonian polity.

The Roots of Prophecy.

The origins of prophecy are largely veiled in mystery, and, so far as we can see, are by no means such that we may recognize them without qualification as the outcome of the authentic religious foundation of Moses. But here, too, we see exemplified a law which is elsewhere evident in the spiritual life. Many a purely spiritual movement springs out of the obscure background of Nature, as, on the other hand, many a movement which has its origin in a higher spirituality is robbed of much of its original purity through contact with the dust and dirt of every day life. Jesus came forward with a high ideal of the Kingdom of God, and what did the church make of it at times? Contrariwise many a lofty ideal is born out of the storm and stress of strictly earthly forces.

The Ecstatics.

When Saul took leave of the aged seer Samuel after having been anointed king over Israel, he was told that he would meet a band of prophets coming down from the high place of sacrifice: "before them resound harp, drum, flute and lyre, while they themselves are in prophetic frenzy. Then will the spirit of Yahweh come upon thee, so that thou shalt like them be seized with the prophetic frenzy and shalt be transformed into another man." The prophecy came to pass.[1] The narrator tells us that as they came to Gibeah a band of prophets met Saul and the spirit of God came upon him, so that he behaved among them as a madman.

The narrative is instructive. It offers the first example of what was known in Israel as *nabi*. For, however much in point of fact we must reckon Moses as a prophet, he is never so called in the older texts. And where the stories of Moses record incidents similar to the above, they can scarcely be regarded as belonging to the ancient tradition.[2] It is clear that this band from Gibeah, in their involuntary manifestation of orgiastic frenzy, resembled rather a band of dancing and frantic dervishes such as can often be seen in the East to-day, than that preconceived notion which we moderns have of prophets. If we compare with our picture that which we derive from many of the words of such men as Isaiah or Jeremiah or even Second Isaiah, there is undoubtedly a very great difference existing between them; yet there certainly must be a bridge leading from one to the other.

[1] 1 Sam. x. 9 ff. Cf. the itinerant Orphic prophets who wandered from town to town in the service of the ecstatic cult of Dionysus in Greece in the seventh and sixth centuries; vide Kern, *Reformen der griech. Relig.* (1918), p 17.

[2] Num. xi. 24 ff.

THRACIAN MYSTICISM.

Widespread through the oriental hither-asiatic world of antiquity as far as Greece, there flourished a peculiar form of *mystical* apprehension of the divine. The merging of self in the Godhead and a mysterious absorption therein became far and wide the inspiration of a powerful religious movement. Where it succeeded in sloughing off its primitive elements, this movement directly gave birth to highest religious values, powerful ideas and personalities.

This was the case in Israel and in Greece. In the latter we see it in the great tragedians and in men like Plato, and in the former in the classical prophets. This inspired ecstatic prophecy would seem to have had its roots in the north, in Thrace and Asia Minor. From thence it probably spread to Syria and to Canaan and on the other side, under the form of Dionysiac frenzy, to Greece; there in connexion with the mysteries it brought about a profound religious development and produced an ethical reform in religion.[1]

In Israel in the days of Samuel this movement under the guise of the *nebi'im* entered into a peculiar alliance with the long established functions of the *seer*. By this amalgamation of two different but nevertheless essentially related forms the movement achieved a significant influence both upon the history of the nation and upon its religious development. It was indeed the germ from which, in course of time, there emerged the greatest development of the religion of Israel, one of the greatest and most unique in the religious history of the world.

[1] See Kern, op. cit., pp. 18, 20. The roots of the movement in the place of their origin must be much older than the period in which we observe the movement in Greece.

THE SEER.

A Hebrew tradition, the accuracy of which can scarcely be doubted,[1] tells us that the native name for the man of God of ancient time was not *nabi*, but "seer". Samuel was still known by that name. The differentia must have been just that state of ecstacy. The influence of the Deity made itself felt not in involuntary frenzy but in this that the seer or oracular priest, called *kahin* by the Arabs, received the divine message in the sacred lot or by various tokens such as the soughing of the wind in the trees or by dreams and visions. This was the form of inspiration in which Moses is supposed to have communicated with Yahweh. But when the seer Samuel introduced Saul into the circle of the *nebi'im*, we may interpret this incident, without detracting from its significance, as indicating that he brought about the coalescence of the ancient office of seer with the new calling of *nabi*.

He must have done this recognizing that this new phenomenon could only be fruitful for Israel, if it were drawn into the service of the Yahweh religion. Whom those bands of ecstatic enthusiasts originally served we do not know. This, however, is assured: we can prove the existence of similar phenomena on Canaanite soil. An Egyptian papyrus of the eleventh century B.C. tells us of precisely similar things on the Phœnician coast.[2] Further, the intimate relationship between the *nebi'im* and the orgiastic worship in Asia Minor and in the service of Dionysus, who is a close parallel with the Baal of Canaan, still further fortifies the view that the whole movement was essentially much better suited to the worship of Baal

[1] 1 Sam. ix. 9.

[2] Vide *Gesch.*, II³, p. 493 (II⁶,⁷, p. 331).

than to the service of the Yahweh of Moses. If it did not remain where it began but could be incorporated into the service of Yahweh without degrading it (of which there was danger), this was only possible on the assumption that some powerful personality took the movement in hand and was able to make it serve higher ends.

SAMUEL.

This Samuel seems to have achieved, and that, too, along the path of patriotism. It was the time of the Philistine oppression; the foreign invaders were flooding the country. The brothers Israel and Canaan hitherto at enmity were now alike threatened not only in respect of their possessions but even of their lives. Just as in the East to-day the Dervishes, unfurling the standard of the Prophet, proclaim the holy war throughout the land, so may those bands of fiercely raving enthusiasts have swept through the land, in their frenzy carrying all before them and preaching the holy war to free their native land from the Philistines. Both sections, Canaanites and Israelites, may have been involved and therewith also the two gods, Yahweh and Baal, or perhaps rather that composite figure of Yahweh-Baal which, at that time, was not unfamiliar. Had there been no powerful determined hand in control, all might have easily served the interests of Baal. Samuel was aware of the situation and laid hold of it. Thenceforth the *nebi'im* became the most enthusiastic supporters and promoters of the worship of Yahweh and those through whom, in the course of time, it was raised to its highest point of development.

SUBLIMATION. NATHAN.

This of course was not possible except by a process of gradual but ever developing sublimation. The frothy and heady wine needed still more careful refining. The details of how this took place and whose work it was we cannot say, but the result of the development clearly proves the fact; and the circumstance that in Elijah we have a conspicuous *nabi* already leading the reaction against the onslaught of Baal worship shows that the development of the *nebi'im* must have set in early in this direction. As is well known, the *nebi'im* in Elijah's time lived together in organized communities which it has been customary to describe as prophetic schools; of the origin of these societies we only know that they were already in existence in the days of Elijah, and by every indication they had a definite standing. So that it is an obvious, constantly recurring and fondly cherished supposition that this association of the unorganized bands into regular fellowship, in which perhaps the beginning of their refinement and purification can be detected, was the work of Samuel.

We have already dealt with the position which Samuel held in other regards. The leading man in the prophetic circle of David's time was Nathan. We can see how he understood his task from his attitude to David's proposal to build a temple and from his encounter with the king after his sin with Bathsheba.[1] The trustworthiness of this narrative has been called in question, undoubtedly on insufficient grounds. Above all we must not lay too much stress on the fact that later this same Nathan played a somewhat peculiar part in the political affairs of the court in

[1] See supra, pp. 86 f.

the king's old age. Here at most the issue concerns the personal character of the man, not his religious office. If the information which we have is to be trusted, it proves that in Nathan, although he was called *nabi*, there came to light few of the qualities of the later prophecy bearing that name. He reminds us much more forcibly of seers like Moses and Samuel; he reckoned the tent and the ark to be the sanctuaries of Israel, and it seemed to him sacrilege to depart from the sacred tradition which had stood for centuries; the supreme law of conduct he held to be the moral principles of the Mosaic religion: "thou shalt not commit murder!" "thou shalt not commit adultery!"

ELIJAH.

After Ahijah of Shiloh whose position is obscure in so far as he, in the name of those faithful to Yahweh and as their spokesman, promised the throne to that man who was destined to strike the strongest blow at the true Yahweh religion,[1] we pass to Elijah and his time. Elijah's battle-cry was: "Yahweh is God!"[2] He lived to wage war against the Baal; he was everywhere where there was a call to withstand the manner in which Ahab and Jezebel sought to gain the victory for the Tyrian Baal. His connexion with the prophetic guilds is obvious. If it is true (a doubt is scarcely possible) that he was the recognized head of those communities, then they also must have been permeated with his spirit. The ecstatic element was still strongly developed in them. In Elijah himself and in his pupil Elisha we still meet the typical features: the master danced before the king's chariot from Carmel to Jezreel[3]; the disciple required

[1] 1 Kings xi. 29 ff. [2] 1 Kings xviii. 39. [3] 1 Kings xviii. 46.

the playing of stringed instruments to transport him into the ecstasy,[1] and his emissary was contemptuously called a lunatic.[2]

On the other hand Elijah's connexion with the Yahweh of Moses was as close as it could well be. In his hour of heaviest oppression he repaired to Horeb, there to meet with Moses' God.[3] And in the slaughter of the priests of Baal at the Kishon [4] we recognize clearly the champion of a God who still bore only too clearly the marks of the ancient jealous God of Sinai. We conclude then that in whatever way we should suppose those guilds to have arisen, and whoever was their founder and first leader, they were developed along such lines that an institution, which in origin was essentially suited to Baal, came to take the field for Yahweh and for him exclusively. Thus an important piece of work was done for the classical prophets. Fundamentally the way was ready for them.

True and False Prophets.

It is not accidental that at this point in the development we are for the first time confronted with a phenomenon which henceforward profoundly exercised the prophetic movement, the contrast between true and false in prophecy. The classical representatives of prophecy was constantly complaining of the obstacles that were placed in their way by many of their fellow-labourers whom they stigmatized as misleaders of the people and false prophets. Now for the first time this opposition appears. Micah, the son of Imlah, a contemporary of Ahab and therefore also of Elijah, claimed that he alone in the

[1] 2 Kings iii. 15. [2] 2 Kings ix. 11.
[3] 1 Kings xix. 8 ff. [4] 1 Kings xviii. 40.

royal entourage proclaimed the truth which was, indeed, bitter to hear. Four hundred prophets testified against him at the king's court; with one voice they held out to Ahab the promise of victory and prosperity; but they were under the control of a lying spirit.[1]

Thenceforth the protest never ceases. Amos was almost ashamed to be called a prophet; he would have nothing to do with people to whom the sacred gift was a craft and the divine mission a means of livelihood.[2] Micah poured forth his biting sarcasm upon men who addressed the people in the interests of their own mouths, who, if anyone refused to throw a bite into their jaws, proclaimed the holy war against him.[3] And Jeremiah complained bitterly of prophets who proclaimed "peace, peace", where yet there was no peace.[4]

THE MORAL CRITERION.

What are we to say of these "false" prophets? It has often been supposed that the distinction has no significance except as a mere party catchword of no importance to history, that the "true" prophets according to the *ex eventu* judgment of posterity came to be simply those with whom in the course of time the majority sided. This is a most superficial view. When we consider how men of the calibre of an Amos, an Isaiah, a Jeremiah threw the whole weight of their moral personality into the scales in support of their words, how Amos suffered ignominious ejection from the land, how Jeremiah endured every insult as a traitor heaped upon him and every suffering in soul and body to the utmost extremity of persecution solely for the sake of truth and of conscience, we

[1] 1 Kings xxii. 5 ff., 18 ff.
[2] Amos vii. 12 ff.
[3] Mic. iii. 5.
[4] Jer. viii. 11, vi. 14.

cannot but come to a different conclusion. When further we carefully examine the behaviour and the principles of their opponents and observe how on the one side appear outward advantage, the favour of the court and of the flattered crowd, on the other side opposition, hatred and persecution invariably attending the appearance of a man, we cannot doubt that beneath possible differences of school and party the decisive difference lay in a profound *ethical* cleavage.[1] On the one side we see gifts, art and profession used as means to a livelihood, on the other the call of Yahweh experienced in the realm of conscience and recognized as a power which bound and constrained to the disinterested service of truth. If we see this opposition appearing for the first time at a point where Baal and Yahweh were beginning to be fundamentally differentiated, and prophecy also in its sphere participated in this process of differentiation, the roots of the opposition are themselves clearly to be discerned within the ranks of the prophetic office. The opposition signifies simply this: on the one hand continuance in the ethically indifferent nature-principle of the ecstatic *nebiism*, on the other hand its compulsion into the service of Yahweh, the ethical God who constrained the conscience of his servants.

The Rechabites and Nazirites.

Closely associated and often working hand in glove with the prophets of this period we meet certain groups which probably had greater significance among the people than the comparatively few references to them would lead us to suppose. These were the Rechabites and the Nazirites. The Rechabites were founded by a man named Rechab, who must have

[1] Cf. Jer. xxiii. 14.

lived in the early period of the northern state and who may therefore have well been a contemporary of Elijah. He may have looked with anxiety upon the religious foundation of Jeroboam I and the bull-worship of Bethel and Dan with its conscious opposition to the Yahweh of Jerusalem. By descent he appears to have been connected with the Kenites who had remained nomads.[1] This explains his position. To him and to his followers the falling away from the ancient nomadic tradition was the root of all evils, a return to the life and the customs of their forefathers would be their solution. With the settlement in Canaan Israel adopted the settled civilization of the country in the matter of agriculture, of building, of vine culture, of industry and commerce, and therewith not only its social and moral implications but also its concomitant indigenous religion, the Baal. Such must have been the considerations which swayed Rechab, as we may divine from the circumstance that Jehu, the zealot for Yahweh, in his struggle against the worshippers of the Baal made use of his close association with Rechab's son Jonadab as a covering for his bloody work.[2] Accordingly we learn from Jeremiah [3] that those reformers and brothers of the simple life, as we should now style them, had raised the repudiation of wine, of house-building and of the planting of vineyards into the position of the first rule of life.

[1] In 1 Chron. ii. 55, the Kinites or Kenites (see supra p. 63) are associated with the house of Rechab. So we understand, following Diodorus (vide my *Gesch.*, II[3], p. 390), they must have the same manner of life as the nomad Nabateans.

[2] He called him to mount his chariot (2 Kings x. 15 f.).

[3] Jer. xxxv. 6 f. The name points to Rechab as the proper founder of the order, but its constitution seems first to have been given it by Jonadab.

Here we have a compact brotherhood in Israel, tent-dwellers, while the Nazirites or consecrated people formed a freer fellowship. They neither lived in tents nor, as far as we can see, in a community. They were united by the common vow. To be sure, this shows that they originated from the same root as the Rechabites. If they did not repudiate tents, they did repudiate wine, that product of Canaanite civilization which was most important and in the baal-orgies most dangerous. Besides this the long unkempt hair was a part of their vow. All this shows their connexion with the nomadic ideal, and the last point indicates their probable origin from a kind of free military association intended to carry on holy wars in the name of Yahweh.[1] We learn from Amos that they were fellow-combatants with the prophets in their struggle against Baal.[2]

The Eighth Century. The Preaching of Judgment.

With a few exceptions such as the time of Jeroboam II the political life of Israel, from the time of Ahab and Jehu until the end of the northern state, presents the picture of the ever crumbling unity and power that David and Solomon had once bequeathed to the State. Furthermore, by the encroachment of the Assyrian world-empire from the reign of Tiglath-Pileser IV, together with the internal strife in Samaria itself, the position of the nation was being increasingly threatened. More and more the fate of both the Israelite states, but primarily that in the north, became a sorrowful but unalterable certainty to those who had insight. At the head of that small company of patriots to whom insight was given stand now

[1] Cf. Samson. So in the Law, cf. Num. vi. [2] Amos ii. 11.

the prophets whose work, from the eighth century onwards, enters upon a new phase.

The certainty that Israel, a dwarf facing a giant, could not hold out against the onslaught first of the Assyrian and later of the Babylonian world-power was coupled in their minds with faith in Israel's status as the people and special possession of God. Only that for the prophets the people was no longer the special possession of Yahweh in a merely external and natural sense as the majority supposed but in the sense of ethical obligation. The prophets came to be persuaded therefore that no one save Yahweh himself had decreed the downfall of Israel and that of course on account of its sins, chief amongst which was the falling away from Yahweh to Baal. The mass of the people in accordance with nature-religion would have seen in their imminent doom, if they had considered it at all, simply the blind sway of the divine indignation, like a fate; the prophets saw in it the national guilt. This was something new. Consequently, as long as the nation continued, the one theme of the prophetic preaching was the constant proclamation of doom on account of Israel's guilt.

Preaching of Hope. Ethical Monotheism.

Side by side with this first certainty stood the equally firm conviction that Yahweh could not for ever and irrevocably repudiate Israel, his special possession. Thus a further element in their preaching came always to be the promise of salvation in some form or other. In part this rests upon ancient traditional expectations, but can by no means be altogether eliminated from the prophetic message. Sin and grace, the downfall of the nation and the prospect the day of redemptive grace thus constitute the two poles round which the prophetic teaching and therewith an important part of the religious thought of the period now revolved.

This realization involves that Yahweh's transcendence above other gods and his ethical qualities of righteousness, holiness, faithfulness and grace now come into particular prominence in the teaching of the prophets. The message of these men was based upon few but great premises, powerful axioms, sufficient to shake to its foundations their people's faith. Yahweh was God of gods and peoples—that implied unqualified monotheism and universalism. Yahweh was a God of righteousness and ethical holiness—that implied ethical monotheism; religion became the root from which ethics sprang. In addition to this the personal, religious significance of the individual life was apprehended with increasing clearness—that implied religious individualism.

Upon these foundation stones was reared the structure of the prophetic preaching. Just as Delphi, Eleusis and the Orphic mystery-cults introduced ethics into Greek religion, so the prophets introduced it in Israel a century or two earlier.[1]

RESULTS.

The consequences for cultus and life followed inevitably. The immediate result of the new times was that the imminent catastrophe brought into prominence the weaknesses in the existing situation and the question, What can be done to mend matters? The answer which commended itself to the people was radically different from that of the prophets. This was the scource of another theme in the prophetic preaching. While to the majority an increased zeal

[1] Cf. p. 125, and Kern, op. cit., p. 7.

for the traditional cultus seemed the way of escape from the troubles of the present, the prophets saw hope exclusively in ethical conduct. With that alone was God well pleased. Their fundamental position was that the true worship of Yahweh involved the purely religious turning towards the true God and the turning away from the Canaanite cultus. The prophetic utterances regarding the cultus are well known. At the same time they provide us with important testimony for the zeal with which the majority set themselves to avert that displeasure of God which the events of the day so clearly portended. Isaiah stigmatized the coming up to sacrifice as a trampling of Yahweh's courts.[1] Amos repudiated Israel's festivals and would have none of their psalms.[2] We can only ask why they made their words so barbed. It is often said that they did this because they repudiated the cultus altogether. That, I think, is incorrect. Much as we may esteem these men, yet they had not yet learnt to worship God in the spirit. We must look elsewhere for an explanation. The cultus as practised in Israel had through over-emphasis upon the ceremonial side sunk to the level of nature-religion. The *opus operatum* is the sign-manual of the heathen point of view according to which the sacred action is the magical instrument whereby a compulsion is exercised upon the deity. Hence the prophets' hatred of sacrifice and even of prayer. Where both proceeded from a sincere heart and were accompanied by upright conduct, they were in the prophets' eyes welcome and necessary expressions of piety.

Hence the consequences for life follow automatically. In demanding righteousness in the place of merely

[1] Isa. i. 12. [2] Amos v. 21 ff.

external ceremonial and thereby giving prominence to the ethical character of Yahweh, the prophets were bound to battle against the ethical and social abuses of the times. With a bitterness, suggestive of modern mass-meetings, they lashed the conscienceless avarice of the rich, the rapacity of the powerful, the exploitation of the poor and economically defenceless.[1] Both state and society were rotten and ripe for destruction. Only, this destruction was not Yahweh's last word but rather the instrument of renewal. Out of the remnant, which Amos and still more Isaiah recognized, a better race should arise in the future.

Amos.

The first in the series is Amos, a sheep-breeder, from Tekoa in the mountains of eastern Judah. Hesiod says of himself that the Muses from Helikon inspired him with divine song; and the shepherd from the poor desert village narrates that in the midst of the great loneliness of the shepherd's life Yahweh took him from the flock and appointed him to proclaim his wrath against the high-placed rakes, the corrupt judges, the merciless usurers and oppressors of the poor in Samaria. Moses also had once wandered in the wilderness following the flock and there had apprehended the voice of God.[2] Solitude and the majesty of nature bring man nearer to God. Amos also suddenly saw visions. Their meaning was that the end of the state, nation and kingdom was come; the punishment Yahweh had visited upon individual places or districts of Israel thus far had been fruitless;

[1] Amos ii. 6 f., iv. 1 f., v. 10 ff.; Isa. v. 8 ff., iii. 1 ff., 8 ff.
[2] Amos vii. 14; Exod. iii. 1 ff.; Amos ii. 6 ff.

a great final harvest day must sweep away Israel itself.[1] Zeal in ritual and in sacrifice could not ward this off; their sacrifices were external. Sacrifice was superficial service, their psalms were meaningless brawling, their holy places shrines of idols.[2] But not Israel alone was involved in Yahweh's punishment; the other nations were no better.[3] And *vice versa* (a thought hitherto not conceived in all antiquity) even Israel's enemies were to participate in the benefits of the universal moral order. Moab was ripe for judgment because it had used lawless violence against Edom which was as much Israel's enemy as Moab's.[4] This is the first trace of international law in history.

HOSEA.

Amos was banished from the country on account of his indignant utterances in Bethel. But his word was not for nought. In the northern state where he had been refused a hearing there arose after him a man of similar force, Hosea. Martyrs have always been sowers. In Greece Hesiod became a poet as the result of his own home troubles. It was the sorrow over his wife's unfaithfulness which made Hosea a prophet. Just as his wife was unfaithful to her vows with him, so Israel had broken faith with Yahweh. Israel was the profligate wife, Yahweh the husband who remained the faithful lover in spite of all.[5] Hosea himself became thereby the prophet of the divine love. Israel's unchastity consisted in the worship of calves and images and in general in all the consequences

[1] Amos viii. 1 ff.
[2] Amos v. 25 f.; v. 5.
[3] Amos i.
[4] Amos ii. 1–3.
[5] Hos. i.; cf. *Gesch.*, II³, p. 509.

of the syncretism of Yahweh-worship with the baal-religion.[1]

> On the summit of the mountains they sacrifice,
> And upon the hills they burn incense,
> Under oaks and poplars and terebinth,
> Because their shade is precious:
> So your daughters commit whoredom,
> And your spouses commit adultery.

And in another place[2]:

> Their mother hath played the harlot,
> She that conceived them hath dealt shamefully:
> She said, I will get me
> After my loves,
> Who give me my bread and my water,
> My wool, my flax,
> Mine oil and drink.

Hosea was a really great poet of much warmth of feeling and inward passion. We cannot therefore wonder at his tender notes when he considers Yahweh's mercy and when ever and again he cannot but give expression to that hope at which Amos had hinted.[3]

ISAIAH.

Following closely on the lines of Amos and Hosea, yet following entirely his own path, the prophet Isaiah made his appearance about 740 B.C. It may be that he was related to the royal house; at any rate he possessed a truly kingly nature, being a royal master alike of language and elevated speech. He received the deepest impression of his life in a memorable hour in the Temple, where, in a trance, he

[1] Hos. iv. 13. [2] Hos. ii. 7. Engl. ii. 5. [3] Hos. vi. 1 ff.

saw Yahweh himself on his throne and heard the words[1]:

> Holy is Yahweh of Hosts,
> All lands are full of his excellence!

This vision gave him the keynote for his message; Yahweh was supreme over all, supreme over his people and the sinful country. Hence destruction loomed inevitably, for Yahweh as judge was preparing a dreadful day of judgment[2]:

> A day hath Yahweh of the hosts
>   Upon all that is high and exalted,
> Upon all the cedars of Lebanon,
>   Upon all the oaks of Bashan,
> Upon all eminent mountains,
>   Upon all exalted hills. . . .
> Upon all ships of Tarshish,
>   Upon all costly finery;
> Humbled shall be the excellence of men,
>   The pride of mankind brought low;
> And exalted shall be Yahweh alone
>   In that day!

When everything was trembling and falling, even the pillars and the thrones, where was deliverance to be found? Such a deliverance there was; the very name of the prophet proclaimed it, for Isaiah means "Salvation from Yahweh". But it did not lie with men, neither could zealous ceremonial achieve it[3]:

> What would I with the multitude of your offerings?
>   Saith Yahweh;
> The blood of bulls and goats
>   I cannot away with.

[1] Isa. vi. 1 ff. [2] Isa. ii. 12 ff. [3] Isa. i. 11 ff.

Nor were agreement and alliance with men of any avail, for [1]

> The Egyptians are men and not God,
> And their horses are flesh and not spirit.

Deliverance was of God alone, and he would grant it to him that had faith. Isaiah thereby first introduced this conception which is the very heart of all higher religions: "if ye will not believe, ye shall not be established". Only he who has trust in God and in the invisible power of his spirit and in goodness, can stand fast when all visible powers are arrayed against him.[2] Herein Isaiah consciously and explicitly makes the whole of life-history, even in the sphere of politics, subject to the great ethical and religious forces, God and the moral order. Only a few indeed would come through this test; *shear-jashub*, "only a remnant turneth", is the name he gave his son.[3] But this small section held the key to the future. When the judgment was past, and the sinful generation done away, then out of the remnant that survived there would arise a new race; its mediator and leader would be the Messiah of the stock of David. Under him would come the age of salvation; justice and righteousness would prevail upon earth, and a divine peace between men and animals would proclaim that Yahweh once again looked with favour upon his people.[4]

MICAH.

Inspired by Isaiah whose fellow-countryman and younger contemporary he was, Micah appeared on the scenes shortly before 722 B.C., from Moresheth, near

[1] Isa. xxxi. 3. [2] Isa. vii. 9, xxviii. 16, xxx. 15.
[3] Isa. vii. 3. [4] Isa. ix. 1 ff., xi. 1 ff.; also vii. 13 ff.

Gath. The most marked characteristic about him was his extremely sharp, masculine utterances concerning the groups of popular prophets previously mentioned [1]—

> Who when they have somewhat in their teeth to bite,
>   Peace they proclaim,
> But whoever thrusts nought into their mouth,
>   Against him they proclaim the holy war.
> And I, even I, am full of might
>   And righteousness and strength,
> To bring home to Jacob his unrighteousness
>   And to Israel his sin.

It stood to reason therefore that in contrast with such fellow prophets he should proclaim woe over Judah as over Samaria [2]:

> So by reason of you must Zion
>   As a field be ploughed, and Jerusalem
> Be a heap of stone, and the mountain
>   Of the Temple a jungle.

Zephaniah.

For a number of decades the voice of the prophets was silent, or, if heard, was violently repressed. In the meanwhile Samaria had fallen, and on the throne in Judah was Manasseh, who was inimical to the prophets of Yahweh and forcibly beat down all opposition. It was not until after he and his son Amon had gone and king Josiah had succeeded, that the preaching of the prophets seems to have regained freedom of action. About this time hither-Asia was submerged by the Scythians, the horsemen from the north, and further indications were not wanting that the powerful Assyrian kingdom was nearing its last days. In this oppressive lull before the storm the prophetic

[1] Mic. iii. 5, 8.

[2] Mic. iii. 12.

movement came to life again. About the year 630 B.C. arose Zephaniah, one of the house of David, perhaps a great grandson of king Hezekiah. In stirring words he described the day of Yahweh which in execution of the wrath of Yahweh was to come upon Philistines, Ethiopians, Assyrians, upon man and beast, upon air and sea, nor should Judah be spared[1]:

> Yahweh hath prepared a sacrifice,
>   Consecrated his guests,
> Then will I visit the nobles
>   And the sons of the king
> And all who clad them
>   In foreign garb;
> I will visit together
>   All who leap o'er the threshold.

NAHUM.

Shortly after him followed Nahum at the time when the Mede Cyaxares had already formed an alliance with the Chaldeans for the final struggle against Assyria. With startling colours and with undeniable poetic power he painted the fate of Nineveh[2]:

> Hark, whip! hark,
>   Rattling of wheels! . . .
> Flaming swords!
>   Flashing spears!
> Slaughtered in multitude,
>   Masses of carrion!
> No end of corses,
>   Men stumble over corses.

Yet as a poet Nahum forgets the proper function of the prophet. Why Assyria must fall we are not

[1] Zeph. i. 7*b*–9*a*. On the leaping over the threshold, *vide* my *Gesch.*, II3, p. 145.

[2] Nahum iii. 1–3.

told, and of Judah's sin we read nothing. Nahum seems rather to be a disciple of the old popular prophets than of his great forerunners and contemporaries—a proof that in these circles, too, there might arise men of lofty spirit and impressive speech.

What is the gain of the prophetic movement thus far? Out of a national God there has developed a God of the whole world and of world-history, out of a cult-God a God of law and of morality. The religious foundation of Moses is saved; indeed, it is transcended.

CHAPTER VI

THE GREAT PROPHETS OF THE BABYLONIAN PERIOD—THE EXILE

MANASSEH.

The religious counter reformation under Manasseh marks the close of the Assyrian period.

In the year 701 B.C. Sennacherib had sent the Assyrian armies to Judah and up to the very gates of Jerusalem. His power made shipwreck on the rock of Zion. Isaiah and his king Hezekiah had experienced Yahweh's greatest triumph. One might expect Yahweh's prestige to be re-established for a long while by this victory over the gods of Assyria and with it the status of the prophetic movement in Judah; but the contrary occurred. Scarcely had Hezekiah closed his eyes when his son Manasseh went over to the other side. It seems that the splendid reputation the prophets enjoyed under Hezekiah was not universal throughout the nation. According to all that we can learn of him from his book, Isaiah was not a man of mere words. When he had the king's ear, as was certainly the case in his latter days, he left no stone unturned to have his demands put into execution. These demands were clear and stern. Thus it was that whatever conclusions we may reach about Hezekiah's reform as described in the Book of Kings, which we shall consider later, during this king's lifetime many aberrations of the popular religion were laid aside and many measures corresponding with the stern and serious moral conceptions of Isaiah and of his disciples were realized.

REVIVAL OF THE POPULAR RELIGION.

The peasant of Judah who had waxed great on his native hill-country as well as the townsman whose father and grandfather in spite of the protests of earnest men offered their sacrifices according to the semi-heathen customs of the popular religion, had little desire to be controlled by the holy men. They would not easily give up the ancient custom of gaiety at the high places and altars, nor the secret arts and devices, household images, amulets, spirits, wise men and women of all sorts, which they enjoyed. Least of all were they in favour of such a serious form of worship as that which the prophets had to offer. We see thus early what Protestantism has constantly been experiencing and is still experiencing, especially in the Reformed Churches, as it stands over against the allurements of Catholic popular religion. It is the hard struggle of a sternly ethical religion which appears to many bare and cold as opposed to a conception which is pleasing both to the senses and to the imagination of many people.

Hence it is altogether credible when we read that Hezekiah's successor Manasseh re-established many heathen and semi-heathen customs in Judah, and that he adopted some new ones. Sorcery and soothsaying, bye-products of the ancient belief in demons, objects of the prophets' particular animosity, again found a champion, as also child-sacrifice which probably dated from a prehistoric period.[1]

[1] 2 Kings xx. See more particularly on pp. 150 f; cf. *Gesch.*, II[3], pp. 570 ff.

Men probably hoped to overcome the dire distress of their time, in which they heard the voice of an angry God, by offering especially terrible sacrifices.[1] It seems that the old half-heathen syncretistic religion, with all its accompaniments of the spirits of the high places and of the fields, sacred prostitutes, sensuous and melancholy customs, was intentionally revived, as if the prophets had never existed. Viewed from this point the much controverted statement that Hezekiah had earlier attempted to make a clean sweep of the high places, *massebahs* and *asherahs*, gains a certain credibility, at least in the sense that he attacked many if not all of them.[2] Only so can we fully understand the counter-movement under Manasseh.

POLITICAL INFLUENCE OF ASSYRIA.

But Manasseh went even a step further; he turned towards the East. Israel for long and even Canaan before its conquest by Israel had been open to influences from the distant East. Babylonian myths and images of gods were known in the Amarna period, and here and there in the Book of the Covenant of Israel's early premonarchic time we hear echoes of the Code of Ḥammurabi. In its struggles in the period of the Judges Israel was entirely occupied with itself. It was developing what it had taken over through the mediation of the Canaanites; new connexions were scarcely made. A similar situation existed at the time of the first kings; for Assyria was far too much occupied with its own affairs to take an active interest in the West; and Israel as a young aspiring state enjoyed the youthful sense of its own powers sufficiently to be self-satisfied.

[1] Cf. Mic. vi. 7, and 2 Kings iii. 27.

[2] 2 Kings xviii. 4. See further, pp. 154 f.

Soon after the collapse of the political unity which David and Solomon attained, the position was automatically changed. After Omri's time Assyria reassumed the old traditional policy of aggression towards the West. Jehu paid tribute to Nineveh; Menahem of Israel and a little later Ahaz of Judah put themselves under the protection of the great king. Hezekiah, it is true, had the great satisfaction of seeing Sennacherib compelled to abandon Jerusalem. But high as were the hopes that welled up in the loyal Yahwists of Judah the political situation remained fundamentally unchanged. On the contrary, after the death of Sennacherib, his son Asarhaddon succeeded in wiping out the father's disgrace and in adding new splendour to the kingdom. His power reached its height with the conquest of Egypt in 671 B.C.

RELIGIOUS CONSEQUENCES.

All these events could not fail to react upon the religious life both in Israel and Judah. According to the most probable exegesis, Amos even shows that his contemporaries worshipped the Assyrian–Babylonian astral deities Sakkut and Kaiwan,[1] but the interpretation of this text as well as its authenticity is a matter of controversy so that we lay no stress upon it here. All the more certain is it that Isaiah could announce that in his time Judah was full of Eastern life; this refers especially to the idols.[2]

There is no doubt that he meant primarily Assyrian gods. This fully agrees with the fact that Isaiah's contemporary Ahaz hoped to impress the Assyrian king Tiglath-Pilezer with his devotion by journeying to meet him when he appeared in the West after the conquest of Damascus and by sending to Jerusalem

[1] Amos v. 26; cf. *Gesch.*, II[3], p. 506[4]. [2] Isa. ii. 6–8.

the model of an altar which he saw there, so that the sacrificial altar of Solomon might be modified in accordance with it.[1] This can only refer to an Assyrian altar and an allegiance to the religion of Assyria. After the conquest of Damascus the Assyrians at once naturally introduced their own cultus there. Accordingly Ahaz seems also to have immediately introduced into Jerusalem the Assyrian star and sun worship with its own priests and even to have maintained sun-steeds in the temple. Obviously Ahaz in his servility purposely treated Judah as a voluntary province of Assyria. The worship of Tammuz, who corresponded to the Adonis of the Phœnicians and probably of the ancient Canaanites, and who symbolized the dying of the spring-time vegetation, is, very likely, mentioned at this time.[2] Here also belongs the arbour which Ahaz erected to the sun-god upon the temple roof.[3]

Manasseh's Counter-Reformation.

Yet all this was wherever possible surpassed by Manasseh. The reforms, so far as we may call them such before Josiah, had intervened. On the other side the power of Assyria had in the meantime attained its climax in the reign of Asarhaddon, so that Manasseh believed he had every reason to outdo his predecessors. Every barrier erected by Hezekiah to restrain Canaanite and heathen influence was surrendered—clearly to avoid bringing the displeasure of his over-lord upon Jerusalem. He particularly hoped to gain his favour by erecting altars for the heavenly host which he placed in the forecourts of the Temple.[4] Ishtar herself, the queen of heaven, as Asherah, will

[1] 2 Kings xvi. 10–18.
[2] Isa. i. 29, xvii. 10.
[3] 2 Kings xxiii. 11 f.
[4] 2 Kings xxi. 3–5.

have taken her place there ; in her train came temple-girls such as in an earlier period had been dedicated to Astarte. In the Temple it was now as it had been at the height of the high place sanctuaries, excepting that instead of Baal and Astarte the Assyrian sun-deities Shamash and Ishtar ruled there. A sun-chariot for Shamash was kept in readiness at the entrance to the forecourt. It was his throne-chariot, with the horses harnessed to it,[1] so that upon it, he, like Zeus in the army of Xerxes, might ride into the field with his hosts.[2] One might suppose that this was intended to replace the ark of "Yahweh of the hosts", if it still existed. The above-mentioned heavenly host in some measure represents the court of the sun-god himself. The astral deities are meant, represented by the various stars and constellations, each claiming its own veneration. Naturally too the cult of Tammuz was revived, and with many other features it persisted through and beyond the reformation of Josiah.[3]

The Babylonian Period.

The collapse of the Assyrian world-empire, long foretold by the prophets of Israel, became a reality in the year 606 B.C. This marks the beginning of the Babylonian period. During this period Judah as a whole underwent a process quite similar to that of Israel in regard to the Assyrian world-empire. More and more the prophets, particularly Jeremiah, became convinced that for Judah also there was no salvation except through the absolute destruction of the State. On occasions this thought had been repeatedly expressed ; now it was uttered in deadly earnest. Much in the prophetic message directly arises from it.

[1] 2 Kings xxiii. 11 f. [2] Enoch vii. 40. Xen. Cyrop viii. 3.
[3] Ezek. viii. 7 ff.

Around the prophets as the representatives of Yahweh gathered small groups of men faithful to Yahweh, men who were animated by the desire to overcome the evils of their time. By this means they hoped, if possible, at the eleventh hour to avert the threatening misfortune. Thus at the end of the preceding and in the course of this period the prophetic Book of Laws was developed. It was discovered in the reign of king Josiah and proclaimed the national law in Judah, Deuteronomy. In it and in the preaching of Jeremiah we find the two most characteristic expressions of the period prior to the Exile.

JEREMIAH.

Of all the prophets in Israel Jeremiah, who represents the transition from the Assyrian to the Babylonian period, is the prophet who approaches us in the most human way. The reason for this is that he more than any other since Hosea, and much more even than Hosea, had the gift of putting his heart and soul into his preaching. His soul was torn in the struggle between what he would and what he must, between personal feeling and desire and the higher obligation that constrained him. The reader experiences all that with him :

> Thou didst entice me ; I let myself be enticed,
> Didst constrain me and hast triumphed.
> I was made an object of ridicule all the day,
> All men make mock of me. . . .
> Quoth I, I will no more think of him,
> Nor speak in his name,
> Then was there within me as it had been fire,
> As a burning in my bones.[1]

If Amos was the prophet of Righteousness, Hosea of Love, and Isaiah of Faith, then Jeremiah was the

[1] Jer. xx. 7, 9.

prophet of religious Personality, of Individuality. He is the man who speaks the language of the heart. To him the individual had an infinite value in God's sight, and he apprehended the relationship between man and God in personal terms. The older prophets had not known this; it marks the dawn of a new era. The watchword of the old prophets had been the "word of God" and nothing more. Their preaching was simply God's word. Now it was "God and I", "God's word through me". Hitherto God's word had been an objective entity; human thought and desire did not enter into the question. Now the subject appears who must accept the message with his own will. By introducing into prophecy the elements of the personal and the subjective Jeremiah became the last of the great prophets, perhaps the greatest. Something had been attained which was supreme, but which was foreign to the nature of prophecy, for prophecy is objective or it is nothing. Thenceforth prophecy had either to maintain itself on this level or abandon its supremacy and be replaced by other movements. The latter was its destiny, but not until through Jeremiah himself it had attained to a further development of the idea of God. If the human relationship to God became a soul-relationship, the barriers whereby Isaiah was still being confined must fall. The Temple and the sacrificial system might vanish; there could be communion with God without them. Herein Jeremiah was the herald of the worship of God in the spirit.

DEUTERONOMY.

For the immediate future the road prophecy was to follow was determined by the second of the two characteristics of our period, Deuteronomy. It appeared in the Assyrian period, but took effect in the Babylonian.

During the great straits to which the towns and the country of Judah were reduced by Sennacherib's invasion of Judah in the year 701 B.C., Isaiah placed all his hope on Zion. Jerusalem could not fall (this was his watchword), for here Yahweh himself had his dwelling-place.[1] Isaiah was in the right. Zion with its Temple as the dwelling-place of Yahweh stood the test. Yahweh himself had acknowledged them. Sennacherib's army had devastated the land of Judah, had burned the towns and with them the local sanctuaries on the high places, but the Temple remained untouched. If Solomon's Temple had previously enjoyed an advantage over those local sanctuaries by virtue of its own magnificence and its prestige as belonging to the royal capital, now its reputation was immeasurably enhanced, and the status of the other sanctuaries jeopardized. Little wonder that they must soon give place altogether to their great rival.

As already mentioned, we are told of king Hezekiah that he abolished the local shrines and that he recognized only the Temple of Zion as the place at which men might assemble for sacrifice. This attempted reform by Hezekiah has been much questioned. But on the basis of the considerations put forward above it appears as almost self-evident that in the circle of the disciples whom Isaiah gathered about him ideas of this kind must long have been current, and that at least after that miraculous deliverance of Jerusalem they were calculated to gain a foothold in the life of the time. The question

[1] Isa. xxxi. 8 f.; cf. *Gesch.*, II^3, p. 562[1].

is of no great importance, for Hezekiah's measures, if they were ever enforced, were by no means thoroughgoing; for under Josiah those sanctuaries with all their paraphernalia flourished anew. So much the more impressive is what was accomplished under king Josiah himself. In the eighteenth year of his reign, 621 B.C., there was discovered in the Temple a law-book upon the basis of which Josiah abolished the high places in the country and centralized all worship in Jerusalem.[1] This measure implied a reform of supreme significance. Had it been merely a question of the abolition of strictly heathen elements, in particular the manifold innovations which had been derived from Assyria, the reformation would very likely have taken its course without great disturbances. But the current religious practices were so completely permeated with wholly or partially heathen elements from the baal religion that the two were no longer separable.

The Reform of the Cultus.

For centuries prophetic men had declared war against Baal and the worship on the high places which was closely connected with the baal-religion. Their words were of no avail. Indeed in Manasseh's time the facts seemed to belie their words. Now, all at once, the prophetic ideal was realized by a revolution of immeasurable importance. The whole of the ancient cultus-life with its unbridled natural instincts and also its often censured aberrations was cut off. Everything was put on a new basis. The priests were left unprovided for, the festivals were dissociated from their origin in the agricultural life, the ancient sacred slaughterings, at each of which the god had

[1] 2 Kings xxii., xxiii.; cf. Deut. xii. 16.

his share, were abolished, and slaughtering was made a secular act. Fundamentally this meant that ancient Israel was buried and Judaism instituted. If we correctly estimate the significance of this act, we must add that had it not been for Deuteronomy and the reformation, ancient Israel-Judah would have come to an end with the Exile, but without any possibility of restoration. This service rendered to the whole movement must the more carefully be borne in mind because later we must deal with its perils.

The Practical Working of the Reform.

At all times and in every sphere human life has been full of paradox. Here we meet with a noteworthy instance; the demands of the prophets are brought to realization by the very men who may rank as the fundamental opponents of prophecy, namely, the priests! It is commonly supposed that Deuteronomy was written by a man in the prophetic circle. This supposition is easily deduced from what has just been said. But when we consider how strongly the concern for the centralization of the cultus in Jerusalem, which is the main point in the law-book, depended upon the co-operation of the priesthood, we are more inclined to agree with those who see in the book the result of the collaboration of both sides, the prophetic and the priestly.

It is also quite natural that the ambitions of the prophets which originally were purely ideal, when they began to find their way into everyday life and when the prophets sought the co-operation of practical men, were stripped of much of their original character. They then came down from the pure ether of the ideal into the realm of the visible, and in this sphere could not remain uncontaminated by contact with the dust of earth and of earthly perplexities. It is certain that Jeremiah, as we already know him, received the new law jubilantly, but soon he retreated and later probably cursed it bitterly.[1] This is more eloquent than any comment.

HIERARCHICAL AMBITIONS.

The old popular religion had broken up the ancient Yahweh of Moses into many local deities. As there was a baal of Mount Peor, another of Hermon, another of Hazor, of Tamar, that is, at a palm-tree, another of Perazim and countless other baals, so the peasant of Israel and of Judah offered sacrifice here to the Yahweh of Mizpah, there to the Yahweh of Bethel or Hebron or Beersheba or Jerusalem. The new law would have all these ideas and their practices absolutely swept away. The ideas of the new law are summed up in Deuteronomy vi. 4, which later became a kind of shibboleth of Jewish monotheism: "Hear, O Israel, Yahweh is our God, Yahweh as One." The saying properly does not express the sole existence but the unity of Yahweh, but in practical life the two came to the same thing. If then the authorities in the State, king and priests, lend their word as law-givers and their strength to carry through this strictly prophetic principle, prescripts such as we read in Deuteronomy xii. 1 ff. and reform movements such as that of king Josiah must result.

The position they held is clearly expressed in the fact that at one decisive point the reform was not carried through as the law prescribed. In Deuter-

[1] See Punkko in *Alttest Studien* (*Festschrift f. R. Kittel*), 1913, pp. 126 ff.; see also infra, p. 160.

onomy xviii. 6 it is provided that the priests from country districts who had lost their livelihood should in future be compensated for their forfeited status by maintenance at the Temple in Jerusalem. This was an honourable and fair intention. The law-giver anticipated that the abolition of the many local shrines would so increase the temple congregations, that the refugee priests could easily be provided for. The priests at the temple were of another mind. The increase in the number of those who came to sacrifice met with their approval, not so however the increased number of priests. The new-comers were summarily excluded from the services of the altar, and the king does not seem to have had sufficient power to insist on the literal enforcement of the law.[1]

The Danger of Externalization.

This throws a vivid light upon one of the dangers with which the work of the reformation threatened the religion itself. Selfishness and mean love of power were probably at work here, as is the way of the world. But they were not necessary to bring this danger to light; apart from them it was already there. With the emphasis laid upon Jerusalem not only as the dwelling-place of God and as the sacred city of the past, but also as the city of the Temple and the priests for the present and the future, the reform became an affair of the cultus and of the priests. There was the inevitable danger that worship should once again be externalized in ways similar to those of the previous cultus which the prophets had severely censured. If the worship of God was centred in one place, it might easily happen that the priesthood with unified and complete control might ascribe

[1] 2 Kings xxiii. 9.

particular value to the cultus as such, and thus the external act might take the place of the inner attitude. Thus in place of a boon a yoke of bondage was laid upon the people.

BEGINNINGS OF THE BOOK-RELIGION.

The second danger lay in the fact that the reform was based upon a book. Josiah called the people together and pledged himself with them to make the newly discovered book from thenceforth the Rule alike for cultus and life. Legal codes were already current; at least the Book of the Covenant was extant in various editions as a book in which the will of Yahweh as *torah* was laid down. But we have no example of obligatory observance enforced by authority, either royal or popular. Custom was observed because it was custom, not because it was written in the law. The written law represented the most general principles for ethical as for civil and religious life. But for the arrangement and ordering of life in detail, especially in regard to the forms of religious ceremonial observance, recourse was had to the verbal instruction of the priest. Whatever of law had hitherto been written, had probably served primarily as providing pattern or principle for the use of the priesthood in their judicial office. Thereby a considerable element of personal and unfettered discrimination was always assured.

Now, on the contrary, there was a recognized law-book in the strict sense of a code, one might almost say of holy Scripture, which was to be literally observed as embodying the law of the State in matters of faith and of life. No one, at least no evangelical Christian, will fail to recognize the blessings to be derived from a fixed rule which in unequivocal terms and through no human mediation tells us what to do and what not to do. But as always happens in the case of a sacred document, here, too, even at the time when it first came to light, there lay ahead the danger that the book itself and letter for letter should be looked upon as an object of veneration instead of a proclamation and testimony of a revelation of the living God in a living act. Unless the greatest care were taken, overnight a book-religion would arise out of a religion of life. This it was that Jeremiah foresaw.

THE EXILE.

In the year 586 B.C. Jerusalem fell into the hands of Nebuchadrezzar. This brought an end to Judah as a State. The upper classes were taken into Babylonian captivity. As far as we can judge, the conditions of the captives were outwardly not altogether unfavourable. True the State was no more, and with it was lost the modest but jealously prized remnant of national independence ; this was for many indeed a cause of bitter sorrow. But a certain degree of civil independence and of personal freedom was allowed the people. If in a letter from home Jeremiah could admonish them to build houses and to buy fields in Babylon and feel themselves at home under the lordship of the great king,[1] and if later Ezekiel could gather his compatriots in his house or assemble them on the banks of a stream, and if, moreover, the captives in Babylon could contribute large sums towards the re-erection of the Temple,[2] all this does not look like confinement and captivity in the strict sense of the term. The main point was that they were deprived of the right to dwell in their

[1] Jer. xxix. 5 ff.

[2] Ezek. viii. 1, xiv. 1 ; Ps. cxxxvii. ; Zech. vi. 10 ff.

native land and of the unrestricted choice of a dwelling-place. They were presumably restricted in their personal freedom to such a degree as the safety of the Babylonian State seemed to require. Otherwise their status will have been that of other colonists from a foreign country. They were under the protection of the Babylonian State, at liberty to hold landed property, to carry on business and in a position to gain considerable wealth. In fact not a few appear to have become prosperous. This of itself explains the apostasy of some. According to the principle *ubi bene ibi patria* many, who were prosperous in their new home, may soon have forgotten the old one. Of these we take no further account.

The Religious Situation. Spiritual Leaders.

Looking at the religious situation, we find that here too the captives were apparently independent and unmolested. A cultus in the old sense was, of course, impossible for them in a foreign country and without the Temple. Often enough had the prophets set before them the prospect of their eating unclean bread in an unclean land,[1] or of their having to live without king and prince, without sacrifice and altar, without ephod and teraphim.[2] All this now actually happened, and for many of the pious it was certainly the severest blow which could strike them. But they still had Yahweh. He was no longer the God who was bound to Sinai or to Zion. Although they longed for Zion and refused to sing songs of Zion in the strange land before profane ears,[3] yet both Jeremiah and Deuteronomy had clearly enough proclaimed that Yahweh was exalted beyond the limits of the Temple. Prayer to Yahweh who was here also in Babylon and

[1] Amos vii. 17. [2] Hos. iii. 4. [3] Ps. cxxxvii. 4.

the congregating of those who clave to him was doubtless unhindered. The picture as a whole is scarcely altered by the isolated jeer of the unbeliever or by occasional persecution or intolerance on the part of individuals.

Apart however from those who became particularly prosperous, there was nothing here to prevent a goodly number, especially the spiritually indolent, of whom naturally enough there were plenty among the upper class who had been taken captive, from a voluntary surrender of their old religion in exchange for the religion of those in power. According to the common opinion of the ancient Orient the religion of the conquerors claimed the victory over Yahweh. Again, others suffered the more from home-sickness and longing for Jerusalem, which they could not forget.[1] Indeed all the more did at least a part of the captive people, which soon came to regard itself as the chosen remnant, feel that Yahweh still had great things in store for his people. They hoped for a national resurrection after the national death,[2] for deliverance and a glorious destiny at the end of the period set for captivity.[3] Indeed Ezekiel in chapters xl.–xlviii. of his book already outlined the new theocratic state with its Temple and its cultus. Deuteronomy and all other codifications that were available were taken up afresh, eagerly studied and revised and then published in a new and enlarged redaction. Also the past history of the nation was now in part retold and in part enriched by the experiences of the immediate past. It was now that they first came to value aright the standpoint of the divine holiness and righteousness for the understanding of their early history. A religious pragmatism was now exercised in the writing

[1] Ps. cxxxvii. 5 f. [2] Ezek. xxxvii [3] Isa. xl. ff.

of history. But it was particularly Second Isaiah who towards the end of the exile gave new life and force to the people's hopes and awakened the belief in the power of divine help in favour of the chosen race. At the same time we can see from his book that that section of the nation which remained faithful to Yahweh and which recognized the destiny of Israel was exposed to much suffering and oppression.[1] These afflictions came only in part from the unfriendly heathen round about them; they also came from their own fellow-countrymen who had grown unfaithful to Yahweh; they reached their climax in the sufferings of the so-called Servant of Yahweh.

EZEKIEL.

This sketch suffices to prove that for the exiles three spiritual leaders were raised up to whom the religious development of the nation was due, the two principal prophets of the period, Ezekiel and Second Isaiah and the Deuteronomic circle.

Ezekiel, who was led into exile under Jehoiakim in 597 B.C., was a prophet of strongly marked individuality. He was the son of a priest, and it may be that he had himself taken part in the sacred ceremonies in the Temple. In consequence of this he has, not unjustly, been called the priest in the prophet's mantle. For together with the prophetic interest the feeling for the cultus was developed in him to a much greater degree than in any other prophet. The parallel between him and Jeremiah is interesting. Jeremiah also was the son of a priest and must, therefore, have had an interest in the Temple and in the divine service. With him it was only a matter of time before the Temple and the divine service would cease to be, but

[1] Isa. xli. 11 f., 14, xlix. 7, lvii. 1; Ps. cxxxvii. 3.

he could do without them. With Ezekiel it was only a question of time before the Temple and divine service would be restored, and he could not do without them. His whole attention was turned to the problem how the Temple and the services in the new Jerusalem should be arranged. This is a characteristic difference between the two prophets born of priestly descent. Indeed it is not merely a difference between the two individuals, but by virtue of the prominent position they held, they developed a difference of tendency and era. The special theology of our prophet is closely connected with this. In his conception of God holiness was the central governing idea, but in a specific sense as the all-commanding greatness and power, so that it was nearly identical with honour and glory, *kabod*. In this setting the holiness of Yahweh was the dominant motive of divine action in Ezekiel's conception. According to Hosea and Jeremiah, Yahweh pardoned Israel for his love's sake, according to Isaiah, if Israel had faith, according to Ezekiel for his honour's sake, that his name be not blasphemed among the heathen.[1] A condition of physical purity was required for presence at the cultus.

From this is obvious his tendency regarding the cultus: such a God would have external recognition of his holiness, would have sacrifice. No wonder, therefore, that his relationship to God is often quite external: on one occasion he eats a book in order to take up into himself its contents, the will of God.[2] Just as the holiness of the creature is conceived as something external or ceremonial, so also the obligations to God so far as they are ceremonial duties. In this respect Ezekiel was the forerunner and pioneer of

[1] Ezek. xxxvi. 22 ff. [2] Ezek. ii. 9 ff.

the period of the priestly rule. This may be regarded as a retrograde step behind Isaiah and Jeremiah, but we must remember that it was, for many, the natural reaction due to the non-existence of the Temple and of sacrifice.

But this does not exhaust Ezekiel's theological character. He himself belonged to two periods, he likewise had two aspects. One belonged to the past, the other to the future. He did not renounce the former; there he stood on the shoulders of Jeremiah. He among the prophets was the pastor.[1] To him the new order was based upon and conditioned by the regeneration of the heart.[2] Herein he was the ethical teacher of the nation with the same earnestness and the same persevering power as Jeremiah or any other of the prophets.

The Deuteronomic Circle.

If we seek to visualize the influences of Ezekiel's work, we must primarily have in mind those circles whose hearts were set upon the preservation and development of the laws concerning the cultus. To them in particular Ezekiel may have been a spiritual leader. A second leader of decisive influence arose for the captive people in Babylon in the circle that had gathered round Deuteronomy. Even before the exile, probably in direct connexion with the appearance of the new law-book, those prophetic circles whose hearts were set on the preservation of the State may have set to work to apply the ideas of the law-book beyond the sphere of ritual reform. Thus arose the sermon-like amplifications to Josiah's book, as we have it to-day, partly as introduction and partly as epilogue to the code.[3] From the same efforts arise

[1] Ezek. iii. 16 ff. [2] Ezek. xxxvi. 26 ff. [3] Deut. i.–iv., xxvii. ff.

the many additions and expansions which we read to-day in the historical books, Judges, Samuel and Kings, and throughout which we recognize the same spirit. How many of these sections were finished before the exile and how many were completed during the exile itself are questions which cannot always be determined in detail, but for us they are of no especial importance. Since the exile witnessed the working out of this process, it will be reviewed in this connexion.

Its Characteristics.

These efforts may be best studied in Judges and in Kings. It is well known that in the Book of Kings after Solomon's death, almost without exception, the history of each individual king is framed in short paragraphs in which, by means of constantly repeated and almost stereotyped phrases, certain information about the individual kings is either prefixed or appended.[1] The most important point for us to notice is the fact that judgment is pronounced upon each king and to a degree his rank is assigned to him in the name of history. If we examine the principle underlying the judgment, it is beyond question derived from Deuteronomy: a king who abolished the high places did that which was well pleasing to Yahweh; a king who left them undisturbed did that which displeased Yahweh. This applies also to periods when the question of the abolition of the high places was never raised. It is thus obvious that we are here dealing with a point of view according to which the real sin of the people and the root of all evil for posterity was the worship at the high places, in par-

[1] Cf. 1 Kings xiv. 19 f., 21, 29 ff., etc. Further xv. 14; 2 Kings xii. 4, xiv. 4, etc.

ticular the apostasy from the Yahweh of Moses. The same applies to the Book of Judges. Here too we find the narratives of the particular judges set in a framework of brief but pregnant sections according to which the success or disaster of the ancient people was parallel to and coincident with their apostasy from Yahweh or their return to him.[1] Other sections by the same school[2] further elaborate these principles and prophets expressly espouse them,[3] so that there can be no possible doubt as to the whole spiritual tendency of the Deuteronomic school. The present suffering, as it was vividly portrayed in the collapse of the State and in the misery of the exile, led the best in the nation to the conviction that the threats of the prophets of old had been fulfilled and that their censure of the national apostasy were justified. The result of the great suffering was to cause people to reflect to a degree hitherto unknown in history. It brought a mood of penitence and contrition which justified the ways of God, and the present generation accepted their forefathers' guilt. Since the sins of the past could not be undone, they wished at least to spare the future similar suffering. Thus the existing texts were taken up afresh, and in them the history of the past was so illuminated that the coming generation might learn what results follow from apostasy from Yahweh.[4] The past was held up as a mirror through which the present and especially the future might learn and take warning. With what thoroughgoing results this was done we learn from post-exilic history.

[1] Cf. Judges iii. 4, 6, iv. 1–3, 23 f., v. 31*b*, etc.; vide *Gesch.*, II³, p. 5.

[2] Esp. Judges ii.

[3] Cf. esp. Zech. i. 4 ff.

[4] Cf. preceding note.

Second Isaiah.

Finally as the third spiritual leader of the period we may rank the great anonymous writer whom by virtue of the place occupied by his book in the canon we usually call Second or Deutero-Isaiah. Even a superficial glance at his book shows that he was more concerned with the above described ideals for the purification and deepening of the religious life of the nation than with the cultus-ideals of Ezekiel. We may take as his watchword the opening phrase of his book: "comfort ye, comfort ye my people".[1] His purpose was to write a book of consolation in which expression should be given to the confident hope of a speedy return to their native land and with it the redemption through the Messianic kingdom. The impulse came from the appearance of Cyrus, in whom he recognized and solemnly welcomed the vessel chosen by Yahweh for the accomplishment of his purpose in Judah[2]; Yahweh loved him, he was his shepherd, his anointed, he led him to victory that he might build Zion and redeem his people. But the redemption which Yahweh had in view was not limited to Judah. Through his people salvation was to come to all nations; the ends of the earth should rejoice in the blessing that came from Yahweh.[3]

But what Yahweh was minded to do Judah would not realize automatically and unconditionally. The proper inner attitude of the people was presupposed, and the prophet conceived it his foremost duty to create this and to assist his fellow-countrymen through faith and penitence to the necessary inner maturity without which no day of deliverance could come.[4]

[1] Isa. xl. 1. [2] Isa. xlv. 1 ff. [3] Isa. li. 4, xlii. 1 ff., xlix. 1 ff.
[4] Isa. xliii. 8 ff., 22 ff., xliv. 10 ff., etc.

It must spread from Israel to the heathen, so that he also became a missionary whose task it was to prepare the heathen for the higher spiritual inheritance which was awaiting them.[1] Thus Second Isaiah's thoughts reached lofty heights. He conceived his God in strictly monotheistic terms. He cast off the isolated limitations still lingering in Isaiah and his successors, so as to apprehend God as the Only one.[2] In distinction from Ezekiel God's justice seemed to him a proof of his love and grace,[3] because to the people under heathen oppression justice seemed a blessing.

As mediator of these great blessings that mysterious figure called by him Servant of Yahweh appears to our prophet. The often attempted interpretation of this figure as symbolizing the whole nation is always met by the obstacle of the thoroughly concrete representation of his sufferings even to death for the sins of others.[4] So he appears as a sin-offering sacrificed for the guilt of his people. But though dead and buried as a malefactor, he did not die as other men but was taken away, "translated", into the upper world as once Enoch and Elijah had been. From thence one day he will return and finish his work, so that kings shall be silenced before him, and he shall divide the spoil with the mighty.[5]

The Effect of the Exile.

Under the guidance of such leaders in a few decades the community underwent a profound transformation. Ezekiel's influence gave birth to the tendency to legalism which won for the succeeding period the name of the age of legalism. The further revisions of

[1] Isa. xlii. 4. [2] Isa. xliii. 11, xliv. 6, xlv. 5, 22 f.
[3] Isa. xli. 2, 10, xlii. 6, xlv. 8 *et passim*.
[4] Isa. l. 4 ff., lii. 13 ff. [5] Isa. liii. 8 ff.

the Law and with it the effort to live apart from the heathen to prevent the old sin of apostasy mark this movement which is particularly distinguished from others by its careful observance of the Sabbath and by circumcision as the hall-mark of the true Jew.

Simultaneous with this movement quite a different one was at work; this was under the influence of those who were disciples of the teaching of Isaiah and Second Isaiah and also of Deuteronomy. Insight into the great guilt of the past as the cause of the present sufferings on the one hand and on the other the never failing home-sickness for Zion, which by loyalty overcame the disloyalty of individuals, together with the preaching of faith and hope by men with the unction of the Spirit—all these things led to the formation of narrower circles of the quiet in the land or "the needy", *'anawîm*. They will have felt that they were fulfilling the ancient promises about "the remnant" which should repent, and were conscious of the duty and the power to be a "holy seed" out of which a new and better race might arise and the rebuilding of the nation be begun. Perhaps their thoughts centred about that Servant of Yahweh whose reappearance they expected.

They laid far less stress upon the Law than upon freedom from it and from all hierarchy; thus there arose a powerful non-legal movement which alongside of the legal movement had a part to play in the future.

In this period of humiliation one fact remains supreme, unheard of hitherto and unique in history for its extent and force, namely, that a people spiritually broken and robbed of all power and all political independence found strength through faith in itself and in its God to aspire to hope for the restoration of the nation.

CHAPTER VII

THE PERSIAN PERIOD—THE JEWISH COMMUNITY

GENERAL OUTLINE.

In the year 539 B.C. Babylon fell into the hands of the Persians. In the very next year, 538 B.C., Cyrus published an edict giving the Jews permission to return home; he also restored to them the Temple vessels which Nebuchadrezzar had carried away in 586 B.C. The return journey took place under the leadership of the first governor Sheshbazzar, who may have been a son of that king Jehoiachin under whom they had been taken into captivity. By his side stood Joshua, a grandson of the last high priest of the old Temple. The returned exiles settled in Jerusalem and its immediate neighbourhood. The ancient capital which had perhaps never been absolutely forsaken was partially rebuilt—without walls, it is true, and at first also without a temple. For the regular sacrificial services a kind of emergency altar was erected on the old site. In the early period of enthusiasm there even arose prophets like Haggai and Zechariah, who urged the rebuilding of the Temple.

Before long, however, a strong sense of disappointment and disillusionment made itself felt. Many of the high soaring hopes which had spurred the returned exiles were not fulfilled. It became increasingly apparent that the nation must accommodate itself to the somewhat jejune existence of a small Persian vassal-state. Apart from internal difficulties there was no lack of external trouble from ill-disposed neighbours. None the less, hope and prophetic vision[1] often soared above the distresses of the moment, and joy at what had really been attained prevailed even amid the present humble conditions.[2]

Soon traces of an undue stress upon the *ritual* side of religion became apparent especially under the sway of Malachi, though the influence of the other prophets exerted a modifying influence. This is explicable not only in the light of the whole previous religious development but also in view of the circumstance that the number of priests amongst the returned exiles was disproportionately large. Meanwhile there set in an undercurrent of thought which joining with the old prophets recognized the essential marks of religion not in ritual but in a spiritual worship of God. This was doubtless further stimulated by a poem which presumably appeared at this time; at any rate it stands in close connexion with it, namely, the Book of Job; quite independent of questions of ritual, it broaches philosophical problems which pierce to the inmost soul far beyond all legal and such-like concerns.

Difficulties Without and Within.

Approaching the details we must first observe that no unanimity has as yet been attained in regard to the *historical* problem of the beginnings of the new community. Still, the above-mentioned points give a view of the situation which may claim for itself the

[1] Hag. ii. 6, 7, 22 ff., i. 14, ii. 3 f.; Zech. iii. 1 ff., iv. 6, 10, vi. 11 ff., viii. 3 ff.

[2] Ps. cxxviii., cxxvii. 3 ff., etc.

greatest degree of probability. For a time a furious assault was made on the authenticity of the edict of Cyrus, but its spuriousness can as little be maintained as the contention that a return in the time of Cyrus did not take place at all.[1]

To be sure, we must give up the antithetical view that throughout the entire exile Jerusalem was uninhabited and offered a kind of *tabula rasa.* The returned exiles probably came back to a city poor in population and rich in ruins, where a community had established itself which found itself in many ways estranged from, if it had not always been a stranger to, the returned exiles.

From this point of view the situation may be considered in detail. The essential features were the internal and external difficulties with which the new community was confronted. Amongst the former the relations of the new-comers to those already in possession were exceedingly troublesome. To begin with, the people in possession of the city and surrounding districts were the remnant of those whom Nebuchadrezzar had left behind together with their descendants. Outwardly these people had beyond doubt made themselves heirs to the properties which by the deportation of the upper class were unoccupied. Inwardly they had not remained what they were, or at any rate they were not what the new arrivals had supposed them to be, for these latter too had not marked time mentally but had greatly changed. One can see how many occasions of friction must have arisen, when the returned exiles set about repossessing themselves of their old homesteads and fields and gardens and found everywhere their rights

[1] Ed. Meyer, *Die Entstehung des Judentums,* 1896; also Kittel, *Zur Frage nach d. Entst. d. J.* (Programm), Leipzig, 1918.

forgotten and their claims lapsed; or when they measured the mentality of those who had remained behind by that which they had attained in exile.

From without, that is, from the outlying population, manifold difficulties arose from the circumstance that the bedouin or half-bedouin tribes of the borderlands, pre-eminently the Edomites, had greedily laid hands on the cultivated fields and meadowlands of Judea.[1] The returned exiles were therefore shut out from large sections of their former territory. This was a source of discord or at least a cause of tension. In the north on the other hand since 722 B.C. the so-called Samaritans, foreign settlers on the soil of the old Israelite State, were so mixed with the older population that both politically and religiously they were regarded and eschewed by the new-comers as a community altogether foreign to them. If we add to all this the depressing political insignificance of the new commonwealth and a number of disasters such as failure of crops, drought and the prostration of trade and commerce, we can easily understand the mood of deep *dejection* which was widely prevalent in Judea.[2]

The Religious Life.

All these circumstances help us to gain a proper understanding of the religious life of the period. Troublesome as external relationships often were, they concealed an element of strength: the hard lessons of the past had been learnt, and there was a willingness to put them into practice. Therein lay a powerful stimulus to action. It was the merit of *prophecy* in its last phase to develop this still further.

[1] In this connexion, see further my commentary on 1 Chron. ii.–iv.

[2] Hag. ii. 3.

The leaders of the prophetic movement were Haggai and Zechariah, later, probably a short while before Ezra, followed by Malachi. The oracular speech of the prophets had been tending to develop into literary addresses; the prophetic consciousness had been growing increasingly subjective. These processes were now advanced up to the point where prophecy in fact came to an end, so that later times only produced a few vague imitators of the prophets. Already Second Isaiah had made a unique distinction between the word of Yahweh on the one hand and on the other a voice from the invisible world that inspired him prophetically.[1] Zechariah went even further: he introduced as mediator between himself and Yahweh an independent person, the *angelus interpres*, as the ancients called him.[2] Man had become so acutely conscious of himself as an independent being over against God that an absolute separation of the two was effected. Hence the Deity was conceived as a Being so *transcendent* that prophecy itself was inevitably dissolved; for a God so transcendent must have priests, not prophets. Thus was the way paved for the period of the priestly rule. In strict accord with this idea of transcendence it was not Yahweh who came to dwell in the Temple but his *glory*. Just as already Deuteronomy had not allowed that Yahweh himself dwelt in the temple but his Name,[3] so here Yahweh was represented by a glorious manifestation, *kabod*; he himself remained in heaven.[4]

Prophecy was becoming book-prophecy; for these writings even more than the earlier books of Ezekiel

[1] Isa. xl. 3: "a voice cried".
[2] Zech. i. 13 f: "the angel who spake with me".
[3] Deut. xii. 5.
[4] 1 Kings viii. 10 f.; cf. Hag. ii. 7 f.

and Second Isaiah were not spoken but were intended primarily for reading; hence prophecy naturally became sacred literature, the object of study for a professional class. The old prophets were studied and developed. We do not know precisely at what period prophetic preaching was displaced by disquisitions upon sections of the existing legal codes, Deuteronomy in particular, and upon the older prophets; but we are led to suppose that this process had already begun in our period because of the stress laid upon its own decadence involved in the facts that Second Isaiah [1] and later the writers of the Persian period expressly refer to the old prophets, and also to the fact that Ezekiel gathered the exiles about him in his house.[2] In any case there was now an energetic development of the study and revision of the older writings which in exile had counted for so much. The contribution of the Deuteronomic school, itself essentially consisting of disciples of the prophets, to the present form of the historical books is signally indicated in the fact that these books were themselves styled prophetic writings.[3]

THE PRIESTLY STATE.

Oral prophecy had been dominant in ancient times, but its day was done, and for both the reasons outlined above its inheritance passed to other movements, on the one hand to literature and literary research, and on the other to the priesthood and the sacred community. It is true that the common people were at first still guided by priest and prophet as hereto-

[1] Zech. i. 4 f., vii. 7.

[2] Ezek. viii. 1, xiv. 1, xx. 1.

[3] The books of Samuel, Judges, Joshua and Kings are called in the Hebrew Bible " former prophets ".

fore[1]; but increasingly, as time went on, the leadership tended to pass from the prophets to the priests. We do not know exactly how the latter moulded the cultus. We expect the influence of the priest to play an important part in view of the developments of which Deuteronomy was the pioneer and also of Ezekiel's efforts which are reflected in the fact that upwards of four thousand priests were amongst the returning exiles. That Haggai and Zechariah attached decisive importance to the restoration of the Temple,[2] we cannot safely ascribe to specifically priestly influences. At that time the building of the Temple was the community's most outstanding concern. Of consequence may be the facts that Joshua the high priest was raised to a position equal to that of the new governor Zerubbabel[3] and the marked stress laid upon the fasting,[4] as also upon the regular sacrificial ritual in the Temple,[5] upon the covenant with Levi[6] and the outward hallowing of the Sabbath.[7] If we reckon, as we may, that one man in ten was a Temple official, we are justified in speaking of a sacred community organized as a *priestly State*. They now only lacked the charter of the constitution, the Law to be interpreted by the scribes.

The Independent Task of Prophecy.

None the less this prophecy still had an independent function. With great earnestness it turned its attention to the present and its peculiar conditions. It never wearied in demanding the re-erection and worthy equipment of the Temple, at the same time

[1] Zech. vii. 3. [2] Hag. i. 5 ff.; Zech. viii. 9 ff. [3] Zech. vi. 13.
[4] Neh. i. 4 ff.; Ezra viii. 21 ff.; Neh. ix. 1 ff.; Zech. vii. 3, viii. 19.
[5] Joel i. 9, 13, 16, ii. 14. [6] Mal. ii. 4. [7] Isa. lvi. 2; lviii. 13.

12

reviving the old promises. The great difficulties which beset the new community both from within and from without, together with much political confusion in the Persian Empire which kindled hopes of the overthrow of Darius, gave rise to feverish excitement; a vast world-wide revolution was expected,[1] and the suspense was almost intolerable.[2] There seemed no doubt that the promised son of David upon the throne of David was none other than the present governor, Zerubbabel, who was of the family of David.[3] Already throne and crown were awaiting him.[4] With the advent of this Messiah would come also the overdue judgment upon the heathen,[5] so that they also would choose voluntarily to join with Judah.[6]

From this alone we can see clearly that it would be a mistake to infer a surrender of the real prophetic spirit from the fact that the prophets worked hand in glove with the priests; at any rate we can emphatically assert that much of the old spirit lived on in these later men. The diligent study of the old prophets kept them from danger. Moreover, that spirit of introspection and self-knowledge, that had developed during the exile and had led to improvement, did not fail to continue its work. Haggai laid stress upon the fact that the unclean had far greater potency of infection than the sacred; "a little leaven leavens the whole lump"; therefore, beware of the leaven of pusillanimity and little faith! That seemed to him the supreme peril.[7] The concerns closest to Zechariah's [8] heart were not fasting and similar usages but the great *ethical* requirements of integrity and

[1] Hag. ii. 6 ff., 21 ff.
[2] Zech. ii. 7 ff.
[3] Hag. ii. 20 ff.; Zech. iii. 8.
[4] Zech. vi. 12 f.
[5] Zech. ii. 1 ff., vi. 1 ff.
[6] Zech. ii. 15, viii. 23.
[7] Hag. ii. 13 ff.
[8] Zech. vii. 4 ff.

love.[1] Elsewhere he urges with the greatest stress that Judah put away sin, and that robbery and perjury meet with their reward[2]; and Malachi, highly as he prized the cultus, would rather see it altogether abandoned and the Temple closed than that the dignity of Yahweh should be affronted.[3]

THE PSALMS.

Although the Temple may after its re-erection claim the chief interest of the period, and although in the eyes of many the cultus might rank as the most important activity of religious life, yet here, too, we must not fail to recognize a parallel movement or undercurrent based upon strictly prophetic ideas. This was associated with the names of the great masters of the past; none the less it was worthily represented in the contemporary prophets. It comes to expression chiefly in the many psalms which date from this period. When the poet of Psalm xvi. could invoke Yahweh in this way: "All my happiness is placed upon thee. Yahweh is the portion of mine inheritance and my cup",[4] he thereby declared Yahweh to be his highest good and bore testimony that the assurance of the grace and fellowship of God was to him more than a happy lot in life; and when an even greater spirit in Psalm lxxiii., after hard spiritual struggles and tormenting doubts, battled through to the confession:

If I have but thee, then ask I nought else of heaven or earth;
Though my body and soul pine away, yet God abideth my refuge and my portion,

he had attained to a victorious assurance of faith exalted above life and death, above earth's sorrows

[1] Cf. Isa. lviii. 5 f.; Joel ii. 13.
[2] Zech. iii. 1 ff., v. 1 ff.
[3] Mal. i. 6 ff.
[4] Ps. xvi. 2; (read kullo 'alèka), 5.

and heaven's joys, which can scarcely be surpassed. These utterances and many like them probably belong to this period; they demonstrate that a close spiritual bond links our period to Jesus and the New Testament.

Job.

A further indication of this is afforded by the powerful poem, Job. If I understand it aright, its author stands closely akin to the poet of Psalm lxxiii.; this it is which determines me to deal with Job here, although there are many arguments for a date either somewhat earlier or somewhat later. The book deals with the problem of the origin of suffering. The dominant opinion, which the prophets still sanctioned, was that Yahweh must upon this earth and visibly requite man according to his deserts. It must be well with the pious; the wicked must meet with mischance. If this did not occur at once, it would happen later; it was certain in the end. Thence it necessarily followed *vice versâ* that unusual suffering could only come upon the man who was loaded with unusual guilt; if a man was overtaken by sudden death or grievous sickness, then he must have been a grievous sinner, else could not Yahweh have so dealt with him.

The harshness, which is involved in this idea, had without doubt long been felt by many, but no one had arisen to contradict the dominant conception and more particularly the point of view of the prophets. Jeremiah and Ezekiel before this had opposed an older idea, a degree more harsh still; before them the saying had been current that the children themselves must suffer with their fathers unto the third and fourth generation[1]; now each

[1] Exod. xx. 5.

man must bear the penalty of his own sin.[1] Therewith justice seemed to be done to the sense of right. Since it was so in general, it was taken for an unalterable principle that God visibly requites and punishes. Men failed to see that it was precisely to the best people that the greatest wrong might thereby be done; and if there was but a single case, yet that one case weighed in the scales as heavy as a whole world—it was a question of the salvation of a *soul*. These were the reflections of the poet. From this standpoint he waged war upon a theory that seemed pious but for him was godless and blasphemous. A righteous man, Job, was involved in grievous mischance. How was such a thing possible? According to the prevailing ideas it was utterly impossible; these are represented by Job's friends. They try to force the unfortunate man to a confession of his guilt. To confute them was at once Job's good right and the task which the poet set himself. He succeeded with increasing clearness; but when that was done, what next? If Job was no godless man, why then his sufferings?

One result, at any rate, the poet achieved: Job's conception of God was higher than that of his friends. The greatness of his suffering brought him near to God, and then he would not let him go again. Even to put the question seemed presumptuous; yet Job could not cease to believe that God would give him the answer; but on earth or peradventure after death? A thought so great that his senses were like to swoon at it![2] But he held fast to it, at least for a moment. The time would come when God himself would bear testimony to his innocence. This was a *personal* solution, but not a solution of the problem nor an answer to his question "Why?" God

[1] Jer. xxxi. 29; Ezek. xviii. 2. [2] Job xix. 25 ff.

taught him resignation[1]: "where wast thou when I laid the foundation of the earth?" Job never got beyond the point where he gives the problem up, and resignation is no solution; but he found the way home to God; suffering taught him to lay hold on God. That was *his* solution.

EZRA. THE LAW.

A new turn was given to the history of post-exilic Judaism by the activity of one of those who had returned from Babylon, Ezra, the priest and scribe. Those who returned to Palestine were only a fraction of the Jews who had originally been in captivity in Babylon. Those who remained in Babylon maintained a keen interest in the experiences of the community in the mother-land; they felt themselves closely bound up with its welfare and took a personal responsibility for its success and progress. This latter appears not to have been thoroughly satisfactory. Quite apart from everything else, the severe pressure of the difficult conditions under which the new community lived makes it very intelligible that complaints were soon heard of a general ethical decline,[2] of the secularization of customs[3] and of the imperilling of the distinctive Jewish tradition through mixed marriages and the incorporation of strangers.[4] It would seem that those away in Babylon did not credit the home community with force enough to bring about a change on their own initiative. Moreover, the actual course of events proves that careful plans had been laid at long range in Babylon with a view to intervention in the mother-land. This was made possible

[1] Job xxxviii. 4.

[2] Oaths taken with levity, Zech. v. 3 f.; perjury, viii. 16 f.; usury, Neh. v.; violence, Isa. lviii. 6 ff.

[3] Isa. lix. 3, 13 ff.

[4] Ezra x. 2 ff.

by gaining favour with the Persian Government through influential Jews resident at the court of the Great King. An edict of Artaxerxes Longimanus permitted Ezra to bring back a further contingent from exile and "with the law in his hand" to scrutinize affairs in Palestine and put them in trim. Ezra's law-book, then, by virtue of a royal rescript became the groundwork of a reform at home.[1] In the main, we should date this somewhere about the middle of the fifth century B.C.

What was this Law and what was its significance? There has been much controversy as to whether the Law introduced by Ezra was the whole Pentateuch or only its most important priestly document, called P. For us the question is of minor importance, for in any case that priestly code was the determinative influence as regards the future. Its introduction was the vital point. We may here also cast aside the much contested problem of the origin and age of particular sections of P. As a whole P is the work of Babylonian Judaism and of that period. It is certain that the work was not prepared without the assistance of earlier material, in parts very extensive material, but it was not these earlier materials but the work as a whole which Ezra now instituted as the Law of the community. As such it was officially published and became the basis of law and custom in the community. As such we must judge it here; for once introduced by Ezra, it from that time onwards fixed the Jewish commonwealth.

Its Idea of God.

If we try to define its dominant ideas, we must put first its thought of God. The whole story is

[1] Ezra vii. 12 ff.

told in the single phrase of the Creation narrative at the beginning of Genesis: "God said . . . and it was so."[1] According to the J document in the second chapter of Genesis Yahweh had taken a lump of earth and moulded it into the form of a man. But in P there is no need of laborious effort and moulding; a single word suffices. Thus Psalm xxxiii. declares, "he spake and it was done; he commanded and it stood fast".[2] Thus the conception was of a God purely spiritual, absolutely almighty and supernal, who ruled over the world and all its powers with sovereign sway needing the help of no mediating activities, who in proud serenity and exalted transcendence remained throned in heaven far above men and mundane affairs. Every anthropomorphic element was accordingly expurgated. In J Yahweh is represented as coming down to earth and walking in the garden; such actions on God's part were unthinkable for P. If a theophany could not be altogether eliminated, it was hinted at, as we have already noticed in Haggai, in such a form that an overpowering light, the glory, *kabod*, of God was substituted for God himself.[3]

In the conception of a God of this highly stressed transcendence and exaltation above the earth it was natural that the idea of *holiness* should play an important part precisely in the sense of that divine majesty which requires that in all their dealings with their God men should pay most deferential regard to his exalted and exclusive nature. We here find developed into a closed system the ideas for which the Holiness-code and Ezekiel had prepared the way. "Be ye holy, for I am holy"; a holy people in the holy land, worthy of the holy God, that is one of the

[1] Gen. i. 3. [2] Ps. xxxiii. 6. [3] Exod. xl. 35.

fundamental conceptions of this priestly code,[1] which was to dominate the whole life of the people in all their relationships, in all that they were and all that they did. So it came about that, under specifically priestly influence and ideas, another ideal was put beside the prophetic ideal of the morality which was grounded upon the moral law, namely, that of ceremonial and ritual procedure based upon the ceremonial law. In the forefront of this stood ritual holiness as Yahweh's requirement. There had been an antithesis between these two even in older times, as we can see from the polemic of the prophets against the excessive importance attached to the ritual of the altar; but now the sacred procedure attained the dignity of a system.

New Life given to Old Rites.

There can be no question that a number of usages inculcated in Ezra's law were not new then or even of Babylonian origin; rather many of them are rites which derived from earliest Israelite or even Canaanite custom and which, stripped in many cases of their original meaning, were here taken over and incorporated into the system. The old usages were far too powerful to be simply set to one side as the more enlightened idea of God would have demanded; so they were rendered innocuous by being forced into the service of the holiness of Yahweh.

Thus circumcision which had originally been a puberty-sacrifice became a sacramental act of purification and dedication; it incorporated into the fellowship of the covenant and involved an obligation to its requirements, Genesis xvii. He who would be a member of the sacred community must bear this

[1] Lev. xix. 2.

mark. In the same way, if a man through contact with the dead or through illness had been rendered "unclean", he must be cleansed again by means of definite transactions before he could be acceptable in the eyes of Yahweh and at liberty to take his place at the divine ceremonies.[1] Certain animals a man must not eat,[2] he must abstain from certain actions which had not the remotest connexion with ethics, if he would not run counter to the holiness of Yahweh.[3] Here we have illustrations of the new lease of life given to primeval customs some of which originally rested upon the fear of demons, others upon obscure *tabu*-ideas. In theory these customs obtained in every period, but in practice there may have been considerable diversity in the manner of their execution. Now their proper meaning was defined once for all.

Positive Requirements.

In these cases we find the dread of the holy God, apart from circumcision, pre-eminently in negatives or abstinences. His holiness also required certain definite services. These are to be traced back to the conviction that ultimately everything in the world, every creature and every possession of man, belonged to God and was only loaned to man. It serves to the honouring of his majesty that in every sphere of life a part regarded as being representative of the whole should be set aside as Yahweh's peculiar possession. Thus in the strict sense all the land was God's possession, but in a narrower sense the sacred place was reckoned to be his peculiar property; in the time of the wanderings this was the tabernacle,[4] in later times it was the Temple and its sacred close. This

[1] Num. xix. 1 ff., 11 ff.; Lev. v. 1 ff.
[2] Lev. xi.
[3] Num. xix. 14 ff.; Lev. xi. 32 ff.
[4] Exod. xl.

sacred place none but the initiated might approach; here alone might the worship of God be celebrated in sacrifice and in rite.[1] Similarly all time, every day and every week, belonged to God, but he set aside for himself definite seasons, Sabbaths, feasts and Sabbatical periods, when the tasks of the ordinary day were laid aside and man gave honour to God.[2] That every possession belonged to Yahweh was kept in remembrance by the setting aside of definite offerings at the sanctuary. Of the produce of the land and of the olive groves and vineyards the first-fruits were dedicated to Yahweh together with the firstlings of the flocks.[3] From the proceeds of commerce and trade there were temple dues as also offerings on every occasion of worship[4]; the offerings of the individual were made as often as occasion might require or means permit, the offerings of the community as a whole at the regular morning and evening oblations and at the festivals. Finally, all human life also was the property of Yahweh. The firstborn had to be redeemed by virtue of certain substitutionary payments.[5] Indeed every male child required such redemption.[6] But within the whole community the priests in particular were dedicated to God and for the humbler services at the sanctuary the Levites; they were Yahweh's particular possession.[7]

Significance of the Law.

In this way the Law presented a well articulated, closed system of sacred requirements, consisting in

[1] Num. xviii. 10, 22; Lev. xvii. 1 ff.
[2] Lev. xxiii; Num. xxviii. f.
[3] Num. xviii. 12 ff., xv. 17–21.
[4] Lev. i.–vii.
[5] Exod. xiii. 1, 12 ff.; Num. xviii. 16.
[6] Exod. xxx. 11 ff.
[7] Num. iii. and xviii.

prohibitions, rites of cleansing and of restitution, and positive requirements of various sorts. Its object was that every member of the sacred people should be constrained to live to some extent in an *atmosphere of holiness.* A citizen of this nation was surrounded and strongly cut off from the heathen world outside by a hedge of legal provisions, so that throughout his life he could not take a step concerning which he had not the assurance of God's good pleasure. The whole of life and all its possible incidental occurrences were safeguarded by rules. Let a man only keep all the regulations, and he could not fail to be a righteous man, *ṣaddīq*, and innocent of offence, *thamīm.* If he made a slip in any particular, provision was made for the possibility of expiation, provided only that the slip was unintentional,[1] for only unwittingly could a pious man transgress such a law; if he did this wittingly, he were unworthy to be called a son of Israel. We observe here all the conditions that require a developed casuistry. If the Law really must keep men from all false steps, there must be no gap in the hedge; that is, the Law must be adequate to every single situation in life. That was only possible if in all cases of uncertainty or in the event of contingencies hitherto unforeseen the correct interpretation and amplification were available. Only then could the Jew feel himself encompassed by the good pleasure of Yahweh, but then absolutely and securely. The former was the function of the scribe, the latter of his successor the Talmudic teacher. From henceforward such

[1] Lev. iv; Num. xv. 22 ff. This was the logical outcome of the system, but in practice it could not be strictly applied. Human nature rebelled against the elimination of every petty theft and deceit; hence we find such compromises as for instance in Leviticus v. 20 ff. and also in Leviticus xvi. 30.

figures present themselves as are indicated in the first psalm, and their importance progressively increases: such was the disciple of the Torah,

> Whose delight was in the law of Yahweh,
> And upon his law he meditated day and night.

The true disciple of the Torah is to this day the man learned in the Torah. To know the Law in all its well nigh innumerable regulations and to apply them to all the circumstances of life is the end of true knowledge, of laborious *study*. Learning became a fundamental requirement of piety and righteousness.

CONNEXION WITH ETHICS.

It is noteworthy that the Priestly Code, apart from the so-called Holiness-code of Leviticus xvii.–xxv., is almost entirely concerned with rites and ceremonies and contains few directions of any other kind. Neither law nor ethics is sufficiently considered. But we may not take it for granted that it was indifferent to them. The complaints of light-hearted oath-taking and perjury, of violence and oppression, which come to us from this period,[1] show of themselves that the moral sense was still alive. It cannot suddenly have disappeared with Ezra's institutions, but this priestly law consciously limits itself to matters of *sacred law*.

The written law was to take over the functions of the priest's former oral instructions; it was to give the layman the key to the understanding of his duty in religious matters. Secular civil justice was the concern of those who judged in the gate, of the elders and the magistrates,[2] and was satisfied by their decisions. For the most part they have no place in P.

[1] Supra, p. 182. [2] Supra, p. 98.

In cases of fraud or assault the decision rested with the magistrate; the Temple and the priesthood had no immediate concern with these; at any rate not at this period. The same applies to ethics. If a man desired to know his duty in the affairs of ordinary life and intercourse with his fellow beings, or what was right and what wrong in a particular case, he would betake himself to the elders and wise men of his town or tribe, or he might turn to prophets as long as there were such. Here also P assumes that general principles are sufficiently clear in the decalogue and elsewhere.

We should therefore scarcely be justified in assuming from P's silence about these things that they were unknown to the authors of it or that they intended to abolish them and put the priestly law in their place. None the less the introduction of Ezra's law did prejudice ethics. We may not accuse P of doing away with but of encroaching upon ethics. The moral sphere was diminished in that ceremonial requirements were ranked beside ethical and apparently made equally obligatory with them. Individual rites were by no means assessed according to their significance for the system as a whole, and the most minute requirement of the ceremonial law was considered as important as the greatest. Above all, the omission of ceremonial duty was made exactly as reprehensible as the omission of moral duty, for the former, too, was held to be completely under the protection and authority of the divine holiness.

Ethics also had no court of appeal beyond this; hence came a depreciation of the supreme authority of the ethical; for if two interests of intrinsically different worth are put on an equality, the one is thereby robbed of its higher worth.

APPRAISING OF THE LAW.

If looking back we seek to appraise this law which became the official rule of life, we shall find its *weakness* precisely in this official character assumed by these regulations, which do not indeed intend to eliminate the ethical side of life, but only deal with it casually and hence put it beside and therefore in practice often beneath that which was primarily near to the heart of the law-giver. Thus henceforward there was impressed upon Judaism a trait of external legality especially in the forms of worship and ceremonial which could not but have important consequences. For persons of weaker character ritual correctness could easily become the matter of primary, morality of secondary importance. It could come about that eating from a vessel that had come into merely external contact with that which was unclean, or eating meat which had not been slaughtered according to the regulations, or the bringing of an offering was considered as important as or more important than unflinching integrity in trade and business or the elementary requirements of the love of neighbour or of parents. A man who closely conformed with the customs of the fathers could thus pass for a "pious" Jew. That he should be of clean heart was desirable, but it was no necessary consequence of his close conformity to the Law.

It is clear that there was imminent danger lest through the multiplicity of legal requirements the ancient ethical spirit of the prophets should be overlaid and ultimately repressed altogether. There can be no doubt that it demanded sacrifice; but we do not know how far the tendency to legality had by this time become uppermost. The fact remains that at this time, whether before or after the activities of

Ezra, psalms could be indicated like those referred to above [1] and also literature could arise like the Book of Job, the authors of which had vastly nobler aims than the external fulfilment of the ceremonial law and meticulous adhesion to the customs of the fathers. This proves that other forces were also at work. A further indication of this lies in the fact that later we find ever and again the circle of *the quiet in the land* who waited longingly for the fulfilment of the Messianic hope and who cherished the teaching of the prophets. So this point of view cannot have absolutely died out during the period under discussion. We have therefore good grounds for assuming that the ethical spirit of the prophets was treasured also after Ezra, though within small circles that gathered about the disciples and spiritual descendants of the ancient prophecy, a stream gradually drying up in the persons of its later representatives.

THE PIETY OF THE LAW.

On the other hand we must recognize the wealth of genuine religious feeling within the sphere of the official law in spite of all its legal narrowness and one-sidedness; this appears alike in the sincere zeal for the fulfilling of the Law as the will of God and in the noble concern for the purity of worship. We should be mistaken if we simply inveighed against the period of legalism as we are tempted to do when we approach the subject from the New Testament. Christians later under the influence of the "law of liberty", as Paul called it, considered the old law an intolerable yoke. Such indeed it would appear to have become in the hands of the later scribes whose casuistry ever contrived new regulations and thereby

[1] Supra, p. 179.

fostered the anxious fear that the Law could never be adequately and completely fulfilled; for when all is said and done, who can make provision for every possible contingency? Justice, however, demands that the more clearly we discover the perils underlying the meticulous scrupulousness in respect of every detail of the ceremonial law, the more stress must we lay upon the fact that within the Old Testament itself that sense of the Law as a burden and a yoke had not yet made itself felt. We do find expressions of *pride* that Israel possessed in the Law a more perfect system of duties and regulations than any other nation on earth[1] and of enthusiastic *delight* in the good fortune of enjoying such a Law.[2] Anyone who has had the opportunity of knowing in our own day the inner life of present day Jewish families that observe the Law of the fathers with sincere piety and in all strictness, will have been astonished at the wealth of joyfulness, gratitude and sunshine, undreamt of by the outsider, which the Law animates in the Jewish home. They delight to read in the Law and to frame their prayers in the terms of its oracles; the whole household rejoices on the Sabbath which they celebrate with rare satisfaction not only as the day of rest but rather as the day of rejoicing. Jewish prayers term the Sabbath a "joy of the soul" to him who hallows it; he "enjoys the abundance of thy goodness".[3] Such expressions are not mere words; they are the expression of pure and genuine happiness and enthusiasm. The psalms mentioned above were written, some of them perhaps primarily, with an eye to such ethical requirements as we read

1 Deut. iv. 8.
2 Ps. xix. 8 ff.; cf. Pss. i. and cxix.; cf. my Commentary, p. 76.
3 Cf. the earlier saying, Isa. lviii. 13.

in the decalogue or in the commandments to love one's neighbour or to be merciful to the poor and oppressed. But it is certain that they have in view not these particulars alone but the whole Law. They prove to us afresh that real profound and earnest piety may lie enshrined in an imperfect setting. All these expressions are, however, only the indication of a soul-consuming fire, a sacred even if perhaps misdirected enthusiasm which was fostered by the Law and was only waiting for the moment of its true direction. Only so can we explain the later history of Judaism, the enthusiasm of the Maccabean period and of the Zealots, the reverence for the Law in the great teachers of the Mishna as in pious Jews of to-day. There was a consciousness that in its Law the nation possessed a great treasure and a feeling that if the Law went by the board the nation too would totter. Here burned and still burns a secret fire that in many cases is only waiting to discover its true fuel. If in the days of Jesus this fire had been coupled with quiet love and with the pure-hearted piety of the "quiet in the land", what an outcome there was bound to be! It would mean that those who had prized the Law above all for its outward ordinances must inevitably have realized that the Law contained other and higher ordinances, and that these derived from the prophets and their ideals.

World Religion and the Law.

Paul's comment upon the Law that it was an interlude is well known.[1] Though this was not the original meaning, our interpretation of Ezra's work is that the Law came at the right moment between Jesus and the prophets.

[1] Rom. v. 20; Gal. iii. 19.

The task which the prophets had set themselves of raising Israel's national religion to a world religion was stopped in mid-course, was indeed shipwrecked. Since the people in exile identified their national uniqueness with their Law, their faith which had been on the road to becoming a world-religion relapsed into a national religion. They became a sacred community with their Law, their Sabbath and their circumcision as their distinctive national marks; that was pure national religion with a sublimated and profounder idea of God. It led inevitably to the repression of those prophetic notions which pointed the way to a world-religion; from the crest of the wave they sank to the undercurrent. The main current was the legal. Under these circumstances everything depended upon the resuscitation and development by another movement of those first intuitions of the prophetic religion which had opened the way for a world-religion. That was only possible if during the centuries of the relapse of the religion into a mere national faith these ideas were kept alive in however imperfect a form. The service of Judaism after the time of Ezra lay in this that it preserved these ideas and handed them down for the new era. In the grand total of the great development of religion in the field with which we are concerned post-exilic Judaism takes the place of the Middle Ages. Just as the service of the Middle Ages to Christian thought in the years between the ancient and the modern world lies in the link that is made possible for us with Paul and Jesus, so the service of legal Judaism to the Israelite-Christian religion lies in the link made possible with the achievements of the prophets. If their achievements had been lost in the often stormy course of the years, then their acceptation and assimilation would also have been lost.

CHAPTER VIII

THE GREEK PERIOD—FROM THE OLD ORDER TO THE NEW

THE PTOLEMIES. THE SEPTUAGINT.

The triumphal campaign of Alexander the Great brought to an end the Persian Empire. He conquered Palestine, and the Jewish commonwealth, probably without noticeable inner changes, came into his power. Judea was hereby incorporated into the Greek world-empire, and from henceforward in conjunction with the whole civilization of the East it became subject to the influences of the Greek culture of which it had hitherto assimilated very little. For Alexander's victorious march to the East brought with it the triumphal march of Greek civilization also.

After Alexander's early death (323 B.C.) Palestine fell to the governor of Egypt, Ptolemæus, the son of Lagus; and Egyptian it remained in spite of many struggles until the turn of the second century. The Jews gladly accepted the Ptolemies as overlords inasmuch as they showed a far greater understanding of the Jewish religion and its peculiarities than did the Greek Seleucids. The Jews had far more in common with the Egyptians than with the Greeks. Particularly in Alexandria, their capital, the Ptolemies at an early date, it seems, vouchsafed great influence to individual chiefs of the Jewish colony. Hence a remarkable synthesis of elements drawn from Greek and Jewish civilizations took place in Alexandria; the most important proof of this for our purposes is the translation of the Old Testament into Greek, the so-called Septuagint. Its first section, the version of the Pentateuch, to which the rest was added in the course of time, we may place in the first half of the third century. Its importance can in no wise be overestimated. The religion of Israel which hitherto had only existed in a language familiar to few, was now translated into a world-language. Suddenly the way was open for its ideas to penetrate into the consciousness of the whole educated world, and this too at the very moment when the victories of Alexander had made the whole world accessible to Hellenism. Jews had long settled in all parts of the world; hence wherever Greek was understood the way was naturally prepared for Jewish congregations and synagogues. Since Hebrew was a lost language to them, they could now gather afresh around their inherited sacred records. The Septuagint thus becomes of importance in world-history. It can be said without exaggeration that it is impossible to conceive Paul as a missionary to the heathen opening the victorious campaign of the Gospel throughout the world of Greek civilization had he not had the Alexandrian translation in hand, nor is the Church history of the first centuries in the form in which it presents itself to us to-day otherwise conceivable.

The Seleucids. The Hellenizers and Their Opponents.

In the year 198 B.C. a battle on the upper Jordan put the Jews under the rule of the Syrian Seleucids. Hellenism had long been accepted in the Syrian cities; indeed they might rank as one of the chief centres of Hellenic life and culture. Owing to their propinquity to Judea and to the Jews' many trade connexions with Syria and the coastal cities, the Jews were threatened by a peril similar to that which had previously come to them from the Canaanites.[1] Many succumbed to it. Greek education was accepted by many Jewish homes and families. With it came also both the rationalizing or spiritualizing transformation of Old Testament notions, familiar in Alexandria but also known elsewhere, and the rejection or sublimation of the traditional ideas of God by the help of allegorical exegesis of the text.[2] Thus it was that not a few lost their joy in the old religion, and therewith they gradually became estranged from the customs of the Fathers. Greek art and Greek science were introduced. Greek life and gay delight in existence lured the people. The upper circles in particular were prone to this apostate tendency.[3] To live and to think as a Greek became the mark of gentility. Josephus tells of Jewish youths who became ashamed of their circumcision and sought to obliterate its marks.[4]

The leader of the emancipated among the Jews was probably Joseph, son of Tobias, whose scandalous life and mean obsequiousness chiefly contributed to estrange the old-fashioned believers from those who were disposed to Greek ways. His son and the priestly family of the Tobiadæ followed in his steps. The zealous protagonist of the other party was the high priest Onias, far-famed for his piety, and the Oniadæ were named after him. So we find the two tendencies organized against each other as two definite

[1] Cf. the anxiety of Jesus ben Sirach, Ecclus. xi. 34, xxxv. 4, etc.
[2] Vide Stade-Bertholet, *Bibl. Theol. d. alten Testaments,* II. pp. 479 f., 356.
[3] Cf. Ecclus. xlii. 2, ix. 16.
[4] *Antiquities,* XII. p. 5[1].

parties, on the one side the Hellenizers or modernists and on the other the old-fashioned believers loyal to the Law, sometimes called the "pious" or Ḥasidim. The difference developed into a desperate struggle through the intervention of Antiochus Epiphanes, who held the throne of the Seleucids from 175–164 B.C. His character was full of contradictions: he was a mixture of romantic enthusiasm for Hellenic culture as a powerful bond to unite his peoples and also of real oriental despotism and moral instability. In one thing only was he firm, in his unconquerable aversion from everything peculiar to distinctively Jewish life. He saw in it nothing but the offspring of haughtiness and obstinate conceit. He had absolutely no appreciation of its historical rights or of its importance. Naturally therefore he took the side of the Tobiadæ, and they for their part did not scruple to avail themselves of his help.

Antiochus' Persecution.

At the command of Antiochus the high priest Onias who was faithful to the Law was first displaced in favour of his brother Jason who was amenable to the king. Citizens of Jerusalem were already making application for admission to the citizenship of Antioch, and Jason sent an embassy with a monetary gift to a feast in honour of Herakles in Tyre. Jews of fashion wore the Greek dress. Indeed in the Greek gymnasium under the fortified castle men of the priestly class looked with pleasure upon the aforesaid conduct on the part of Jewish youths. But Jason too was soon forced to give place to Menelaus, one of the Tobiadæ. Menelaus, it is true, was soon ejected again, but he was reinstated by Antiochus. Without protest he permitted Antiochus to enter the Temple and rob it of its best treasures. Two years later (168 B.C.) his emissary Apollonius even transformed the fortress of David into a Syrian garrison-post with the definite purpose of arresting the Jewish opposition to Hellenism on the spot where it had its roots in the Jewish religion and its peculiar usages. Sacrifice and circumcision were made capital offences, the celebration of the Sabbath and of feast-days was interrupted, the altar of burnt offerings was polluted by placing upon it a vessel for offerings to Zeus of Olympus—perhaps to Antiochus himself. If anyone was found even with the Book of the Law in his hand, capital punishment was the penalty.[1]

Antiochus had judged the Jews as other peoples of similar numbers and their God as one amongst the other gods. He had no conception of the fire that burned secretly in the soul of the Jewish people. He was soon to realize that the Jews had a faith and a God for whom they would suffer and die. Out of a people who for centuries had not carried swords there arose suddenly, the moment their ancestral faith was jeopardized, an army of Crusaders. True, the representatives of the Hellenizing priestly aristocracy, with Menelaus of the Tobiadæ at their head, acquiesced after the opposition between the king and the people had come to the point of a struggle for national existence. The faithful on the other hand gathered around the venerable country priest Mattathias and his five sons to do desperate battle for life or death. With prayer they entered the fray,

> The praises of God upon their lips,
> A two-edged sword in their hands.[2]

[1] I Macc. i. 45–49. [2] Ps. cxlix. 6.

THE MACCABEES.

The fellowship of the pious, the Ḥasidim, who hitherto had stood aside as the "quiet in the land," now took a keen interest in public affairs. Many others joined them. After Mattathias' death his son Judas the Maccabee took over the leadership (166 B.C.). In an incredibly swift campaign he succeeded in mastering the Syrians. The Temple cultus prescribed by law was restored, the polluted altar was rededicated. Moreover in 162 B.C. after several reverses he succeeded in wringing from the Syrians the right to the free exercise of religion. Thus the unequal struggle was ended by the triumph of the Jews against the attempt to Hellenize them perforce.

The struggle had hitherto been for the faith and for the Law, but in the sequel it more and more developed into a duel between the Maccabees, now known as Hasmoneans, and their rivals for power. Since Jonathan, Judas' brother, had become leader, temporal power was the only matter at issue. At first they succeeded in acquiring the high priestly office; the attainment of the commandership in chief and princely rank soon followed. Aristobulus even took the title of king. Thereby those who hitherto had been the champions of the faith no longer differed from ordinary rulers whom they emulated in military exploits, in luxury and domestic policy. Their rule was less and less based upon popular approval, so much so that many felt a sense of relief when Pompey brought the unworthy game to an end and incorporated Judea into the Roman empire.[1]

THE TEST OF THE LAW.

In the process of development which has here been outlined one point first of all stands out with par-

[1] Ps. Sol. ii. 7, viii. 19.

ticular clearness: we see the significance of Ezra's institutions. Ezra's desire was fulfilled, and it brought forth its fruit. He gave to his people a Law which should guide them through life. He himself, even in his most sanguine dreams, can scarcely have imagined that it would have this effect. Apart from the above-mentioned psalms in praise of the Law[1] we have little if any direct evidence for the period between Ezra and the Maccabees. But its lack is amply compensated by the Maccabean revolt. Their struggle was simply for the Law and its cultus. Before battle was joined, the rolls of the Law were spread out before God[2]; battle was waged strictly in accord with the Law. That is only conceivable on the supposition that what Ezra had desired and attained for his own age was continued after his death, and in the two intervening centuries had so taken root that the attempt to tamper with it could be considered equivalent to an attempt to rob the people of its most holy possession, indeed of its very soul. Thus the experiment was definitely brought to the issue, and the proof given how little up to this time the Law was felt by the majority as a yoke and a burden.

THE TEMPLE AND THE PRIESTS. THE SYNAGOGUE.

The firm position which the Law had acquired demonstrated that the institutions of the Jewish commonwealth, unpretentious as this commonwealth was in comparison to the former national organization, was yet fundamentally sound at heart. Authority was in the hands of the governor or his representative together with his ministers, the elders, who later developed into the Sanhedrin, so far as mundane

[1] See above note 2, p. 193. [2] 1 Macc. iii. 48.

matters were concerned, such as taxes, the judiciary, public order, the army. By his side stood the high priest [1] as the supreme authority over the Temple, the temple-dues and the sacred matters. Meanwhile the more the community made up its mind in earnest to renounce political ambitions and to develop into a religious community, the more the Temple and the priests naturally gained prominence. The Temple, so long as it stood, at any rate until the advent of Christianity, remained the real centre of Jewish life, primarily of course of the religious life but also in a general sense of the national life. We get an idea of the tremendous concourse of the pious from all parts of the world at the great feasts when Josephus speaks, no doubt with great exaggeration, of three million people.[2] We have many proofs of their enthusiasm. The reverence for the priests and the high priest kept pace with the reverence for the Temple. Their influence increased constantly. In the Greek period the high priest was even entitled ethnarch, and the priestly nobility about him often ruled the people.

What the Temple was in Jerusalem, the synagogues were to the Jews outside, at first among the Diaspora, where it probably had its origin. The first tentative beginnings may perhaps reach back into the exile, where the pious gathered about Ezekiel in his house and out of doors beyond the city by the running stream.[3] Positive evidence for the synagogue we find first under Ptolemy Euergetes,[4] shortly after 250 B.C., then in Psalm lxxiv. 8, which most probably dates from the Maccabean period. Beyond doubt the

[1] Zech. iv. 14, vi. 13.

[2] Bell. Jud., II. xiv. 3; cf. VI. ix. 3.

[3] See above, pp. 160, 176.

[4] Vide Schürer, *Gesch. d. Jüd. Volkes*, II[4], pp. 499 f.; Stade-Bertholet, *Bibl. Theol.*, II. p. 338.

synagogue was then soon introduced into the motherland. The more the reading of the sacred Scriptures and their interpretation together with prayer and blessing became a part of divine worship, the more urgent did the need become for local places of prayer everywhere outside of Jerusalem.

THE SCRIBES.

This was naturally a breaking away from the priesthood. Since sacrifice was only offered in the Temple, the teacher of the Law, the scribe, was sufficient for the synagogue. Ezra, the father of this order, had still been a priest; so no doubt were many others after him. In the course of time the offices of scribe and priest naturally were sundered. The scribe was a sort of lay religious teacher, as in olden days the prophets had been. When the Maccabean struggle attained the victory of the Law over every assault, the position of the scribe was naturally strengthened. The morbid elaboration of casuistry, of which amusing examples are recorded,[1] may be connected with the increase in their numbers. But when this lay teacher came forward as a man of learning, a new class was formed in distinction from the unlearned laity. It consisted not of priests nor yet of mere laymen; it was the learned teacher or Rabbi. Beside the priest came the learned theologian; in addition to the Temple and beyond it beside the synagogue was the house of instruction.

The scribes were, first and foremost, teachers of the Law. But the Law which since the time of Ezra had become entirely canonical did not exhaust the inherited literature. The task of sifting the existing literature and of connecting with the Law all that

[1] Bertholet, op. cit., p. 338.

seemed to have permanent value remained. At the same time all that had not yet been put in writing was recorded, thus making an addition to written literature. This was the origin of the Canon. The standard by which the materials were judged may appear strange to us. But it was the necessary result of the dominant ideas of the time. Whatever in the opinion of the period was valuable for edification was included; the rest was put on one side. The prophetic canon may have arisen about 250 B.C., that of the Hagiographa in the last two centuries. The nature of the contemporary literature is indicated by such books as the Biblical *Chronicler* and others of which we shall immediately treat.

THE LITERATURE. THE PSALMS.

Literary productions as well as institutions and personalities are always the surest indications of intellectual life. That there was no lack of these in the period under discussion is shown by the almost modern complaint of one of its representatives, although a late one and probably not with exclusive reference to Jewish literature, that " of the making of books there is no end ".[1]

Sacred poetry, begun long before, now made rapid progress. Psalmody, which was in the hands of the Levitical choral families, was most intimately connected with the Temple, twice restored, once after the exile, once again after the Maccabean wars. It is still an open question how far psalms and hymns similar to them were employed in the synagogue prayers. At any rate the whole treasury of sacred song, so far as it was available in any century of our period, served the community in whatever was vital

[1] Eccles. xii. 12.

at the time. Only one must not conclude from this that all those songs originated at this time. Old songs were adapted for the service of the present, songs that were originally purely personal expressions of individual feeling were adapted for corporate worship. The circles of those who were faithful to the Law preferred and composed new songs to glorify the Temple, the cultus, and the Law. Those who were emancipated from the Law uttered warnings against valuing the cultus too highly and recalled the prophets of old or spoke of sin and grace and faith and trust in God and fellowship with him as if there were no such thing as the priesthood, and as if in all these matters man had no need of human mediation. Those in particular whose souls were full of the Messianic expectation gave utterance to their emotions in sacred poesy. That the perils and victories of the Maccabean movement should give fresh impetus to psalmody is only what we should have expected. Although we do not know to what degree this was the case, it is very probable that a number of psalms, amongst which Psalms cxlix., lxxxiii. and lxxiv. are prominent, must have originated amid the storms of this heroic age.

PROVERBIAL WISDOM.

The teachers of Wisdom still more clearly than the Psalter considered as a whole show us a strongly developed piety that was emancipated from the Law even in the days of the Law's dominance. It seemed best to speak of the Book of Job earlier. The Book of Proverbs is closely allied with it. There were at all times in Israel, as we know was also the case outside of Israel from antiquity, teachers of Wisdom who loved to clothe the message they would impart to their disciples in the form of proverbs, particularly those containing a comparison.[1] Quite credible is the tradition that even Solomon had a part in proverbial Wisdom and introduced it into Israel.[2] It is thus by no means impossible that in the older sections of the canonical Book of Proverbs there are genuine proverbs which date back to Solomon and Hezekiah and their circle, as the book itself supposes. But the book as we have it belongs to our period, in particular the first section of it, chapters i.–ix., which in part consists much less of proverbs than of an educational treatise. This is suggested alike by the rationalizing of ethics and more especially by the personification of Wisdom. Closely associated with this also is the section, chapters x.–xv., in which the doctrine of retaliation and the contrast between the pious and godless is strongly emphasized. These passages are peculiarly significant as throwing light upon the spirit which dominated individual circles in this and the immediately preceding period.

Even in ancient days and outside of Israel, particularly in Egypt, there was an order of wise men. They may have been closely related to the scribes.[3] In distinction from the sacred ordinances of the priest the wise man was exercised in purely mundane prudence, as in matters of etiquette, of self-protection against strange women, of respect for those in authority. So in Israel there probably was from antiquity in the keeping of laymen such a Wisdom

[1] Cf. "as is the man, so is his strength"; "let not him that girdeth on his armour boast himself as he that putteth it off" (Judges viii. 21; 1 Kings xx. 11). Hence the name *mashal* = "proverb", strictly, "comparison".

[2] 1 Kings v. 11 f.

[3] As regards these latter in the early period, see my *Gesch. d. V. Isr.*, I³, p. 196 (I5,6, pp. 155 f.).

which had no connexion either with the official priesthood as trustees of the religious learning or with the prophets as the unofficial, free, moral religious teachers of the people. In the canonical Book of Proverbs we find clear traces of this secular lay wisdom. It recognizes no national boundaries, but is frankly human and international. Its exponents are in fact described as north Arabian kings, Agur and Lemuel, but they might just as well have been called the famous wise men of Egypt, Eni or Ptah-hotep. But the book contains even more: it also recognizes an order of religious lay-teachers, who have nothing in common with the scribes referred to above. They might rather be considered as the immediate heirs of the prophets now extinct. They were not scribes, and their standpoint differed widely from that of the scribes because they were not in sympathy with the cultus; they scarcely refer to it and in general proceed as if there were no such thing as Temple or sacrifice. With all the more urgency they strove to attain followers for their ideal wisdom, and enticed others to taste its blessings. None the less they were far removed from being purely theoretical "wise men", philosophers. Because they were unecclesiastical, they had no thought of being irreligious as well. Rather, religion was the foundation of their Wisdom: "the fear of God is the beginning of wisdom".[1] Thus they were lay-teachers after the manner of the prophets of old, but in very different times and surroundings. Like the prophets they were independent of the cultus, and like the later of them their concern was rather with individuals than with the mass, but they lacked the prophets' fervour of utterance and their ecstasy of soul. Like the prophets they pointed men

[1] Prov. i. 7.

first and above all to God, but in distinction from the prophets they did this rather upon the basis of prosaic every-day wisdom. The high ethical exaltation of the prophets became proverbial prudence and popular wisdom.

ECCLESIASTES.

If the influence of Hellenism can scarcely be denied in the Book of Proverbs, it is yet more clearly manifested in Ecclesiastes. Little as the doughty realism of Israelite thought was prone to speculation, so little could it in the end remain altogether unaffected by Greek philosophy. It is remarkably significant that the first and only attempt really to align the one with the other led to an impossible result. The book was written by a man who had come to grief through Greek wisdom. He had heard of it or read about it, and what he heard and read went to his head: "it all made me as silly as if a mill wheel were going round in my head". Recent expositors have thought they have discovered the solution of the riddle by their favourite formula of interpolation. It is indeed possible that here and there a sentence was added later. But the real truth about the Preacher is not to be explained in this way; he adopted all sorts of ideas that were new to him, and he could not assimilate them. Hence he is tossed about hither and thither between epicurean hedonism and sceptical pessimism, between pious resignation and blind fatalism. The book reminds one of the Talmud; the voices of the Rabbis in the Talmud the one saying this, the other that, correspond to the mutually antagonistic notions of the new wisdom and the ancestral religion in the Book of Ecclesiastes.

JESUS SIRACH.

After this unstable swaying hither and thither with its end in a weak compromise it is a relief to find in Jesus Sirach a man who knows his mind and takes up a definite position as opponent of the new wisdom. This son of Sirach (about 180 B.C.) openly avows himself an enthusiastic venerator of the Law: "be not ashamed of the Law of the Most High and his commandments; let all thy discourses be occupied with him."[1] His fiftieth chapter is an enthusiastic hymn to the high priest and the glories of the Temple worship. His ideal is *Wisdom*; but there is no doubt what manner of wisdom he means; it is the wisdom of the *scribes*, and his house was little else than the school-house.[2] All, it is true, may share in wisdom, but those who fear Yahweh possess wisdom from the cradle.[3] Hence too all the wisdom of Greece cannot equal the Law of God. In that wisdom he sees "manifold conceits of the children of men".[4] As his wisdom accords with the Law, so Jesus Sirach gives evidence of an advance beyond the Book of Proverbs also in his attitude to the cultus.

In contrast to Proverbs he highly esteems the cultus, ultimately not from inward constraint but for the sake of the law, "because the Law ordained it".[5] The same is true likewise of good works.[6] Yet (as practical as are many of his regulations) he descends in respect of motive a step lower to humdrum expediency and sheer self-interest.[7] His frankness is

[1] Ecclus. xlii. 1 f., ix. 16.
[2] Ecclus. li. 23, vi. 36 f.
[3] Ecclus. i. 10, 14.
[4] Ecclus. iii. 23 f.
[5] Ecclus. xxxii. 6.
[6] Ecclus. xxix. 9.
[7] Ecclus. xii. 1 f., xxxviii. 18, 21, xxii. 23. Mourning for the dead is bad for health (xxxviii. 21).

refreshing, but in the spirit of this legality of the scribes there is little that uplifts.

APOCALYPTIC.

The son of Sirach like all of his period was acquainted with the Messianic expectation, but the little use he makes of it corresponds with his dispassionate manner no less than with the comparatively peaceful epoch of the Seleucid domination. His interests lay in the present. All the higher rose the excitement some decades later when Antiochus had let loose the storm which drew the eyes of the Jews involuntarily away from the cares here below to the help from above and away from present distress to the promised future. The stress of the period again begat prophets, but they no longer had the force and original freshness of the old prophets. They like those were visionaries, but at the same time they possessed a kind of science of the interpretation and unveiling of the secrets of ancient prophecy and, in general, of matters pertaining to the world beyond. Enoch, one of the new prophets, even called himself a scribe; another borrowed the name of Ezra; we call them revealers, apocalyptists; we distinguish them from the prophets of old because, to be sure, they confined themselves to the words and images of their predecessors, and even developed them, but they frequently displaced the ethical feeling of their predecessors by ingenious speculation and grotesque phantasy. Their origin dates from Ezekiel and Zechariah. In the peaceful period of the fourth and third centuries they did not flourish. From the time of the Maccabees however they reappear. Their most distinguished exponent who may here act as their representative is Daniel.

DANIEL.

The main section of the book, the apocalypse proper, chapters viii.–xii., appeared during the fearful persecution of the period.[1] Here the seer longingly directs his gaze inward and upward. Above all the calamity of the present and all the violence of men stands the secret of the eternal reign of God. When will it come and how? The "man in whom he is well pleased",[2] the chosen one, can fathom the problem. He hears it with fasting, sackcloth and ashes,[3] indeed greatly agitated, pale and disfigured and prostrate on the ground.[4] Then he hears that all that is now occurring under Antiochus Epiphanes was long ago predetermined and therefore had to come to pass as it has. On Nebuchadrezzar followed Cyrus and the Persian Kings, after the Persians Alexander and his successors, one succeeding another, till finally there appears a bold and quarrelsome one, who "stands up against the prince of princes, but without man's hand shall he be destroyed".[5] He wars against the king of the South, that is Ptolemy VI, "and his armies desecrate the sanctuary, the citadel, and cause the daily offering to cease and the abomination of desolation they set up".[6] All this comes as it was bound to come, and thereafter comes the end.

He had learnt from Jeremiah that the redemption was to come after seventy years. Seventy years were long since passed, but rightly understood they were seventy weeks of years, and they fell into three divisions of seven, sixty-two and one week of years; in the two

[1] To the same period belongs the closely allied animal-apocalypse in the Book of Enoch.

[2] Dan. x. 11–19. [3] Dan. ix. 3. [4] Dan. x. 8, 10.

[5] Dan. viii. 23, 25. [6] Dan. xi. 25, 31.

halves of the last, its three times and half a time, destiny was to be fulfilled.[1] A fearful affliction such as has never been before and surpassing all previous experience will come through the dreadful One. But Michael, the prince of the angels, will come to the help of the people, and whoever is inscribed in the Book of Life shall be saved. The martyrs shall live again, and " the wise and they that turn many to righteousness shall shine as the light of heaven ". Unhelped by any the oppressor shall be overtaken by death[2]; or, in another form, a heavenly court of justice is gathered, an Ancient of Days, the Eternal God, sits on his throne surrounded by thousands of angels; the book is opened, and the fourth beast, the Greek Empire to whom the Man of Enmity himself belongs, is consigned to the flames; but one " like unto a son of man " comes with the clouds of heaven; he appears before the Ancient of Days and is here endowed with the eternal dominion over the peoples, the Messianic Empire.[3] He to whom the roll of Messiah is here ascribed is neither a man nor the people but an angel-like being, more like an angelic prince such as Michael

The Parties.

Our period is also particularly marked by the party politics within the community; this was also in part true of the foregoing period. Even in the Exile, under the influence of the prophetic and in particular the Deuteronomic movement, certain circles of the pious had been formed. They continued into the post-exilic period alongside of the official Church and seem to have ranked as the defenders of the non-legalistic piety and also of the Messianic expectation. They seem to have been drawn in particular from the

[1] Dan. ix. 21–27. [2] Dan. xi. 45, xii. 3. [3] Dan. vii. 13 f.

lower economic and social ranks, and they called themselves therefore "the poor", *'ebyōnīm,* and "the needy", *'aniyīm.* After the exile these two words cover the same ground as pious and well pleasing to God; they involve therefore an ethical religious idea. The exilic community or its pious core ranked as a community of the poor and oppressed or meek, *'anawīm.* And on the other hand, as the external differences between the pious and the godless were more developed and both names came to be used technically of movements, the pious voluntarily took the name of the needy.

Contemporaneous with this development or slightly subsequent to it there was another; the pious more and more broke away from the godless in outward matters also; hence diverging movements were formed. The manifold contact with foreigners and foreign life, whether with Babylonians, Persians or Greeks, inevitably involved the danger of outside influence. The party strictly loyal to Yahweh, which under these circumstances necessarily came to be the legalists, consciously gathered in opposition to those who were sympathetic towards heathen customs and were ready to make a compromise with the world outside; and inasmuch as the latter belonged rather to the ruling and possessing classes, the identification of the pious with the poor was natural. The course of the development in the one case was different from that in the other. We now find springing out of an opposition of direction an ethical-religious opposition between the pious and the godless. How far-reaching this opposition was we can see from the fact that each party was organized against the other as a closed community,[1] and that hostility and

[1] Ps. i. 1, 5, lxiv. 5.

persecution of the one side by the other was not infrequent.[1]

Ḥasidim and Phil-Hellenes.

The opposition existed previously, particularly after the advent of Hellenism, but it was in the Maccabean period that it became acute; now we have on the one side the pious who call themselves the community of the *ḥasidim* or Hasideans,[2] the believers of the old school, true to the nation and the Law, and on the other side the phil-Hellenes and modernists whose party name we do not know. The former, as the "quiet in the land",[3] kept themselves aloof from the noisy doings of the world; but in the days of the sorest need they came out of their retreat and enthusiastically took up arms. They are spoken of in Psalms lxxiv. and cxlix., the Book of Daniel and the beast apocalypse in Enoch. The phil-Hellenes appear as turn-coats and godless persons who must be exterminated. The Maccabean war inevitably brought the one party to the support of Antiochus, the other to that of his opponents.

The victory of the Maccabees meant the overthrow of the phil-Hellenes; and so long as the victors remained loyal to their religious duty, the *ḥasidim* stood by them. But the war soon developed into a struggle for temporal power, unintelligible to the pious. That snapped the cord that bound them to the Maccabean lords, and the breach was widened in proportion as their successors, the Hasmoneans, became mere worldly rulers. According to Josephus[4] it came to a formal breach under John Hyrcanus. At any rate it is at this time that we first find the

[1] Ps. v. 7, 11 ff., x. 14 ff., lvii. 7.
[2] 1 Macc. ii. 42; Ps. cxlix. 1.
[3] Ps. xxxv. 20.
[4] XIII, x. 5 f.

name Pharisees, that is, the set apart, the Separatists, applied to those hitherto called the pious or *ḥasidim*. Their opponents are now called Sadducees. The former name is derived from the Hebrew word *parash*, separate, since they fundamentally repudiated and opposed temporal interests in the priestly, that is, the spiritual rulers. The latter name comes from Ṣadok or Ṣadduk, formerly head of the temple priesthood. With this they marked themselves as the party of the priestly aristocracy which was at the same time that of the rulers and therefore of the worldly aristocracy emancipated in respect of the Law and temporal power. Thereby the situation was fundamentally changed; the rulers who had been the protagonists of strict obedience to the Law had become the representatives of the party of freedom from the Law, not the religious but the worldly; and the pious who had once been the great supporters of the ruling powers had now become their embittered opponents, not on the ground of politics but of religion. In opposition to the secular politicians attired in the vestments of religion stood the pietists and those true to the religion of the Church.

Sadducees and Pharisees.

The Sadducees and the Hasmoneans seem constantly to have grown closer together. Hence Enoch in reference to them speaks of kings and rulers,[1] the rich and the haughty.[2] They were the representatives of the Hellenistic Illumination,[3] "children of the earth", children of this world who would know nothing of the Beyond and of the resurrection.[4] Besides this they were profaners of the sanctuary and adulterers[5]; at

[1] Enoch xxxviii. 5, liii. 5. [2] Enoch lxiii. 10, xcvi. 5 f., xcviii. 2.
[3] Enoch xciv. 5, xcix. 2. [4] Enoch c. 6, cii. 3, 6 ff.
[5] Ps. Sol. i. 8, ii. 3, i. 7, ii, 11 ff.

this time they were openly referred to as godless.[1] In contrast with them the Pharisees were "children of heaven",[2] the righteous,[3] they of the resurrection,[4] but also the sponsors of the fearful judgment awaiting the godless[5]; one would do well therefore to cut adrift from these latter[6]; it were better to escape with one's life into the desert than to lapse into their godless ways.[7] This attitude enables us to understand how the Pharisees came to welcome the end of the Hasmonean domination even at the price of foreign invasion.

One may comment adversely upon the external and partisan use of the terms "pious" and "godless" and upon the narrowness and self-satisfaction of Pharisaic thought, but there can be no hesitation in answering the question upon which side was to be found more of real religion and a more earnest zeal to please God. Had it not been for their proud aloofness from "publicans and sinners", due in part to their connexion with the scribes, their ostentatious display of piety and their over-narrow, fine-spun legality which cramped them, it is certain that Jesus would not have had only words of reproach for the Pharisees, as he certainly found more than one Nicodemus amongst them. The Sadducees produced neither a Nicodemus nor a Gamaliel nor a Saul.

But above all we must not forget that through all this time to the very last, alongside of the Pharisees of conspicuous piety like the above-mentioned, there was the group of the "quiet in the land". To this circle belong the aged Simeon who was eagerly looking for the consolation of Israel and for the day when he should see the Saviour sent by God, Anna,

[1] Enoch xciv. 5, xcix. 2; Ps. Sol. i. 1, ii. 16, etc.
[2] Enoch ci. 1. [3] Enoch xciv. 1, 4, xcix. 10; Ps. Sol. i. 2, iii. 3 ff.
[4] Enoch li.–liv. [5] Enoch xcvii. 3 ff.; Ps. Sol. iii. 9 ff.
[6] Ps. Sol. ii. 34. [7] Ps. Sol. xvii. 15 ff.

eighty-four years old, who gathered about her all those "who were looking for the redemption", and others such as the disciples from Emmaus who hoped for the Redeemer of Israel. To this circle also belong those called blessed by Jesus in the Sermon on the Mount, whether they be called the poor or the mournful or the persecuted or the pure in heart or they who hunger for righteousness; to it belong also those to whom he spoke at Nazareth and to whom as the poor and oppressed he announced "the acceptable year of the Lord". They constituted a noble army of those who quietly waited and eagerly looked for God's hour. They belonged to none of the usual parties or movements; they quietly pursued their way. But they were at hand, as soon as he should appear in whom they saw their hope fulfilled.

Expectations of the Future.

The expectations of the future to which we are naturally brought may form the conclusion of our sketch. The older expectation presented a two-fold picture: on the one side there was a popular, nationalist hope of the future, on the other a hope deepened by the prophetic spirit and containing elements of a cosmological expectation which perhaps were derived from foreign sources.[1]

These two sets of ideas remained, but they developed into a predominantly nationalist hope on the one hand and on the other into a hope of far wider scope, universal and apocalyptic.

The period of the return from exile and of the attempt to constitute the new community under the pressure of the yoke of foreign dominion had given a strong impulse to the old national hope. Haggai

[1] For the beginnings, see above, pp. 107 f., 111 f.

and Zechariah thought to lay hands upon the coming Messiah in the person of Zerubbabel.[1] After that for a long period there are no definite occasions to which we can point. Assuredly the expectation did not lie dormant, but it may have been confined to a small circle. The storms of the Maccabean period awakened it to new life in a form which we can clearly grasp. We have fairly rich material for the elucidation of our problem if we may take for well grounded the present tendency of many scholars to ascribe to the Maccabean period a large number of psalms and texts from the prophets. But in view of the uncertainty of the dates of many passages it will be wise to reserve judgment. Still the psalms yield extensive material either for the pre-Maccabean or the Maccabean period; to these we must add for the later centuries Daniel and Enoch and for the last century before Christ the Psalter of Solomon.

ESCHATOLOGICAL PSALMS.

First of all there peremptorily appears in those psalms which are probably to be ascribed to the Greek period the hope, nay the tempestuous demand, for the Last Judgment.[2] After it Yahweh himself will ascend the throne and enter upon his rule over all the world. Enthusiastic odes of triumph herald this event and the dawn of another age therewith.[3] Then also will judgment be exercised upon the heathen; indeed, God will pour out his wrath upon them and take dreadful vengeance on them.[4] Hereupon the Messiah will appear, assume the rule over the people of God and extend his sway to the world's end. This is the setting of such psalms as the lxxii. and ii., or

[1] Hag. ii. 20 ff.; Zech. vi. 9 ff.
[2] Ps. xliv. 24 f., cxliv. 5 f.
[3] Ps. xcvi. 10, xcvii. 1, xlvii.
[4] Ps. lxxix. 10 ff., cxlix. 7 ff.

passages such as 1 Samuel ii. 10, if they properly belong to our period. But even if they were already extant, then like Psalm lxxxix. 20 ff., where prayer is offered for the fulfilment of the promise to David, they were sung at this time with peculiar significance. Hitherto we have been speaking on the whole only of nationalist expectation. Such indeed was the rule, but on closer inspection we find not a few songs in which purely *religious* ideas beside and beyond these others have an important place. Psalm xlvii. 9 f. will serve as an example of this: here the nations worship Yahweh as a single people of God; thus they have been incorporated into a community of those who believe in Yahweh. Here Israel's pride is no longer the outward triumph but the victory of the cause of the true God. Similarly in Psalm xcvii. 6 ff. we pass from the outward manifestation of Yahweh to the religious advantage of his coming: the noblest treasures of the new Kingdom of God are the true knowledge of God and the victory of righteousness.

Enoch.

We have seen Daniel's attitude toward the expectations of the future and how he reached it by the idea of the "one like a man." A similar tendency is expressed in certain sections of the Book of Enoch, a document in which we find the utterances of a whole group of apocalyptists of different dates after the beginning of the second century. In the so-called "beast-apocalypse"[1] which dates from the time of Judas Maccabeus the pious appear as lambs. But they grow horns; the gentle *ḥasidim* take up arms. The master of the flock, however, seats himself upon his throne for judgment. The godless shall be burnt in the fiery

[1] Chh. lxxxv.–xc.

lake.[1] After that a white bull is born with great horns, the Messiah.[2] As we see, it is all to be accomplished within the limits of national life and earthly conditions, and the Messiah only appears at the end, the ideal ruler of the redeemed community, to be sure, but without having ascribed to him a particular rôle or any clear relationship to Judas, the sheep with the great horn.[3] The so-called " weeks-apocalypse " goes a step further.[4] In the eighth week the righteous are given the sword to execute judgment upon the godless. But after that in the tenth week, reaching far beyond the previous limits of temporal events, there will appear a new heaven. " Then come endless periods of goodness and righteousness, and sin shall no more be thought of for ever."[5] Here there is introduced a trait that is thoroughly transcendental and at the same time ethically spiritual. This is developed further by the " Similitudes ".[6] In the second of these the seer beholds the judgment upon the godless and the resurrection of the dead. The final assault of the world-powers is wrecked upon the rock of Zion. Then one ascends the throne " with venerable head white as wool ", and with him is one " whose countenance is like that of a man ", the Son of Man with whom dwells righteousness.[7] He will be the light of the nations and the hope of sorrowful hearts; his name was named before the stars of heaven were formed.[8] If hitherto the Messiah was mentioned almost solely because of the traditional scheme, here on the contrary (for only he can be meant by Enoch's Son of Man) he is represented as having a great and ideal purpose. It sounds as if one

[1] Enoch xc. 26. [2] Enoch xc. 37. [3] Enoch xc. 9.
[4] Chh. xciii., xci. 12–17. [5] Enoch xci. 17.
[6] Chh. xxxvii.–lxxi. [7] Enoch xlvi. 1–3. [8] Enoch xlviii. 3 f.

were listening to Isaiah when his work is described as a reign of righteousness, or to Second Isaiah whose Servant of the Lord breaks not the bruised reed and brings light to the heathen.

Psalms of Solomon.

The Psalms of Solomon belong to the last century before Christ. The more clearly the real nature of the Hasmonean kingship was revealed, the greater was the longing for the fulfilment of the ancient promise. It came with renewed force when, under Pompey, Jerusalem fell into the hands of the heathen. Even the momentary joy of the Pharisees over the fall of their enemies could not blind their eyes to their humiliation:

> Look down, O Lord, and let there arise for them
> Their King, the son of David!

So here again the Davidic King of the prophets takes the place of the Son of Man or the bull with great horns.[1] Their feelings are expressed in the exclamation,[2]

> Blessed he that liveth in those days,
> To see the salvation of the Lord!

Jerusalem must be purged of the heathen and the godless; the survivors will be Jews loyal to the Law. To them are added the Jews without, for the heathen will submit to the sway of the Messiah and bring these with them.[3] Since he is innocent of sin, God's power supports him.[4]

Jesus.

Two leading thoughts with alternating force dominate Judaism after the Babylonian captivity: the Law and the Messiah. Now one is in the foreground, now the other. Increasingly a link between the two

[1] Ps. Sol. xvii. 21.
[2] Ps. Sol. xvii. 44.
[3] Ps. Sol. xvii. 21–32.
[4] Ps. Sol. xvii. 33 ff., xviii. 6 ff.

was forged by the pressure of the age and by the spiritual domination of the Pharisees: the Messiah appears as the ideal of those faithful to the Law. Thereby indeed the best element in the Messianic idea and that which properly was in accord with the prophetic teaching in it was jeopardized. If Jesus came forward with the claim to be the fulfiller of the Messianic expectation, his first task must be to gain the victory for its higher, purely religious side. This side was not forgotten amongst his contemporaries, for the Similitudes of Enoch do not long precede the oldest of them such as Simeon and Anna; but it was all the more in his mind in proportion as he lived in the prophets and derived from them a very different significance than most of his contemporaries with regard to the Servant of the Lord who had long come to be thought of as one with the Son of David and the Son of Man.

He appeared then amongst his people with the call to repentance, because he realized the nearness of that Kingship of God of which the Old Testament had so often spoken, and with the Kingship the New Age. Let him, who as citizen of this coming Kingdom would share in its blessings, prepare his heart. For it is a Kingdom of spiritual blessing, not of this world, and its King, the Messiah, is a King of truth and righteousness. Only he who is of pure heart may see God, and only he who hungers and thirsts after righteousness may be filled. Those who were righteous of themselves and satisfied he rejected; only him who came to him weary and heavy laden would he refresh and redeem.

Jesus lived and moved in the Old Testament. Whatever was permanent in the Law and the prophets, whatever was of eternity in the history or teaching or poetry of Israel, that he adopted and developed, and in taking to himself the title of the Son of Man he clearly connected himself with Daniel and Enoch. Therefore he did not refuse to call himself or to allow himself to be called by the further titles of Son of God and Son of David, that is, the Davidic Messiah.

The Old Testament is therefore summed up in him. There was nothing truly great there which he did not adopt and represent in his own person. For he was not a teacher as others had been. What he taught, that also he lived. He not only pointed the way; he was the way. Hence men were either on his side or against him. And there is nothing that belonged to Jesus which was not to be found in the Old Testament in some form, in perfection or in its beginnings. Both belong together. Jesus going back behind Judaism took over the prophetic conception of God. He brought to light again what Isaiah says of faith and works. What the best of Israel's poets had sung of suffering and the highest good resounds in his teaching, where he sets the Kingdom of God and his righteousness above all the riches of the world. And when the prophets of Israel made the Messianic salvation transcend the boundaries of their own people and embrace all the world, here too we have exactly his own thought, even though not a word of his precisely to this effect has been preserved. Nothing was further from him than an emphasis upon an exclusive nationalism. When the poets of Israel with increasing clearness speak of the "poor" and "needy" as those to whom the future belongs, he knows that his true congregation was in their midst, for theirs is the Kingdom of Heaven.

So we understand that he knew himself to be the One in whom the age was fulfilled. Whoever recognizes the justice of this claim will not hesitate to recognize that the Old Testament and the religious history of His people was like himself, God's own work.

INDEX

PRINTED BY UNWIN BROTHERS LIMITED, LONDON AND WOKING, GREAT BRITAIN

GEORGE ALLEN & UNWIN LTD.
LONDON: 40 MUSEUM STREET, W.C.1
CAPE TOWN: 73 ST. GEORGE'S STREET
SYDNEY, N.S.W.: 46 CARRINGTON STREET
WELLINGTON, N.Z.: 4 WILLIS STREET